F

Preschool Children and Free Play

Fiona Rowlands

Preschool Children and Free Play

Educator Attitudes towards Free Play and
Preschool Children's Free Play Opportunities

VDM Verlag Dr. Müller

Imprint

Bibliographic information by the German National Library: The German National Library lists this publication at the German National Bibliography; detailed bibliographic information is available on the Internet at http://dnb.d-nb.de.

Cover image: www.purestockx.com
Published 2008 Saarbrücken

Publisher:
VDM Verlag Dr. Müller Aktiengesellschaft & Co. KG , Dudweiler Landstr. 125 a,
66123 Saarbrücken, Germany,
Phone +49 681 9100-698, Fax +49 681 9100-988,
Email: info@vdm-verlag.de

Produced in Germany by:
Reha GmbH, Dudweilerstrasse 72, D-66111 Saarbrücken
Schaltungsdienst Lange o.H.G., Zehrensdorfer Str. 11, 12277 Berlin, Germany
Books on Demand GmbH, Gutenbergring 53, 22848 Norderstedt, Germany

Impressum

Bibliografische Information der Deutschen Nationalbibliothek: Die Deutsche Nationalbibliothek verzeichnet diese Publikation in der Deutschen Nationalbibliografie; detaillierte bibliografische Daten sind im Internet über http://dnb.d-nb.de abrufbar.

Coverbild: www.purestockx.com
Erscheinungsjahr: 2008
Erscheinungsort: Saarbrücken

Verlag: VDM Verlag Dr. Müller Aktiengesellschaft & Co. KG , Dudweiler Landstr. 125 a,
D- 66123 Saarbrücken,
Telefon +49 681 9100-698, Telefax +49 681 9100-988,
Email: info@vdm-verlag.de

Herstellung in Deutschland:
Schaltungsdienst Lange o.H.G., Zehrensdorfer Str. 11, D-12277 Berlin
Books on Demand GmbH, Gutenbergring 53, D-22848 Norderstedt
Reha GmbH, Dudweilerstrasse 72, D-66111 Saarbrücken

ISBN: 978-3-639-04125-5

Introduction

The purpose of this research is to examine teacher's attitudes towards play and children's free play opportunities in child care centres. According to research, 44% percent of 3-to 4-year-olds were involved in some form of an early childhood education program in 1989, including preschools, daycares and home-based daycares and preschools in the United States (Schwienhart, 1989 cited in Summers, 1991). The numbers are similar in Canada and have risen. In 2001, according to Statistics Canada, over 50% of all Canadian children were being cared for by someone other than a parent. Twenty five percent of those children were in a daycare center. In all the provinces there was a substantial increase in the number of families utilizing daycare services. In 2000/01, 41% of children between the ages of six months and five years were in daycare. By contrast, in 1994/95 only 25% of children in this age group attended daycare. The amount of time children spend in daycare it is important to consider the role of teachers. Teachers have always played a major role in socializing children. As more and more children are placed in daycares at earlier and earlier ages the impact that teachers have may become even more significant. The attitudes that teachers have towards children's play may also impact on how teachers choose to structure the daily routine of their classrooms. The purpose of the present study is to examine teacher's attitudes towards free play and how they impact on children's free play opportunities.

Defining Play

Prior to discussing any aspect of play it is important to clearly define play. Rubin, Fein, and Vandenberg (1983) state that play is difficult to define since the word covers a broad range of ideas. They discuss the possibility of eliminating the word play and focusing attention on a narrower range of categories. Another issue raised by Rubin et al.

(1983) is societies' attitudes towards play. They point out that play has a negative

reputation in North American society because it is seen as being in opposition to work.

There are various forms of play and there are numerous definitions of play. In general

play can be defined as "creative, original, innovative and imaginative" activity (Bruce,

1993). More specifically it can be defined as "a range of simulations within a time

continuum, including the influences of materials, social relations, real-world experience,

and decisions about what to stimulate." (Reifel & Yeatman, 1993). Bruce (1993) adds

that play involves the child using skills that he/she has, or is in the process of acquiring.

Klein, Wirth, and Linas (2003) mention another characteristic of play, which is that

children must enjoy an activity for it to be characterized as play. In his definition, Slavin

(1988) also includes positive affect as a criterion, which is as follows:

> Play is voluntary, pleasurable, spontaneous, and self-initiated
> Play involves repetition or elaboration of behaviours already acquired, but it also
> promotes new skills and abilities. Play is pursued "for its own sake"; it is not goal
> directed. Play is creative and nonliteral. It contains elements of reality interwoven
> with fantasy. Play changes as children develop. (Slavin, 1988).

Rubin et al. (1983) discuss six factors that have been agreed upon by a number of

theorists, which describe play. The first characteristic is that the behaviour must be

intrinsically motivated. If a child is engaging in an activity for any reason other than

his/her own pleasure then he/she is not playing. The second characteristic of play

behaviour is that the child focuses on the process and not the product of the activity. A

child engaged in an activity where he/she is focusing on the goal is working and not

playing. The third characteristic of play behaviour is that children ask the question,

"What can I do with this object?" If a child is focusing on determining what an object

can do, and the characteristics of the object, they are exploring the novelty of the object.

When a child knows what an object can do and he/she is able to focus his/her attention on what he/she is able to do with the object, he/she can play with it. The fourth element of play is that there is a level of pretense involved. Children must use their imagination at some level. For example, a child who is stacking blocks together is exploring the blocks. A child who is pretending the blocks are pizzas and is putting them in an oven is engaged in play. The fifth component of play is used to distinguish play from games. This characteristicstates that for a behaviour to be classified as play there can be no rules that are placed upon the children from external sources. For example, if children are playing hockey with blocks and marbles and they establish the rules of their activity then they are playing. If an outsider tells them what the rules are, the activity becomes a game. The final characteristic of play is that the child must be actively involved. A child sitting and staring off into space with an activity sitting in front of him/her is not, by definition, playing.

As stated by Rubin et al.(1983) many theorists have agreed upon the characteristics that they put forth. Therefore, for the purpose of this paper play will be defined as any behaviour which meets the criterion put forth by Rubin et al. (1983).

Many people feel that children spend a substantial amount of time playing. When one considers the definition put forth by Rubin et al. (1983), it becomes clear that a substantial amount of play time cannot truly be classified as such. Coupled with the fact that children's play time is decreasing is the fact that the value our society places on play is declining. These ideas are discussed in the next section. Also, in the next section of this proposal the problems related to the perception of the value of play will be addressed.

Problems in Play Opportunities

According to one researcher (Jambor, 1996), there are five societal trends that are endangering children's right to play in the United States and to a degree in Canada. The first issue addressed by Jambor (1996) is the fact that neighbourhoods are becoming less safe. People do not know their neighbours as well as they used to know them. North American communities are more transient, people are working longer hours and there are more households with two working parents. All these facts help create environments where (a) children need others to care for them and, (b) crime may become more prevalent. As neighbourhoods become less safe, parents are less likely to let their children play outside. The second issue Jambor (1996) discusses is the fact that our society, as a whole, is becoming less and less physically active, which is supported by recent statistics that show that the rate of obesity, due in part to poor eating habits and a lack of exercise, amongst adults and children is increasing (www.statscanada.ca). The decline in physical activity outside of school is further compounded by the third issue addressed by Jambor (1996), specifically schools are reducing the amount of playtime for children in favor of more structured, teacher-directed activities. Another issue is that more parents are divorcing and remarrying, this means that children spend more time shuffling between one home and another. This may reduce the amount of time available for them to play and also to establish relationships with neighbourhood children. The final issue Jambor (1996) discusses is that people are more concerned with safety and less concerned with the value of play. As our society becomes more concerned with keeping children safe, many play behaviours are not allowed as they are deemed to be unsafe (e.g., playing outside unsupervised). This issue impacts preschool and daycare educators who often bend to parental pressure to forbid children from engaging in any play behaviour that they consider dangerous.

The issue of school curricula that devotes less time to play has an impact on early childhood educational programs. As elementary school curricula focus more on academic skills, parents want their children prepared for school by the early childhood education centers. Thus, parents pressure early childhood educators to focus on academics as opposed to just letting the children "play" (Charlesworth, Hart, Burts, Thomasson, Mosley, & Fleege, 1993). Many educators, who believe play is important, find it difficult to maintain their position that play opportunities are necessary with the pressure from parents to create an academic structure in their classrooms. This idea is also reinforced by Hatch and Freeman (1988) and Klein, Wirth and Linas, (2003). The fact that it is much easier to determine if the preschool prepares the children academically makes it far more appealing to many individuals (Egertson & Isensberg, 1987) than trying to determine what children are learning through play. In contrast, Hatch and Freeman (1988) found a discrepancy between early childhood educational theory and the educational practices described by teachers, principals, and supervisors. The individuals interviewed by the researchers stated that they were concerned with preparing children for the academic content of first grade. The kindergarten classes were mostly skill-centered, academically-oriented programs.

A study (Rothlein & Brett, 1987) found that parents did not condone their children spending a substantial amount of time playing. They felt that children should spend no more than 30-50% of their time engaging in play. Another study (Egertson & Isenberg, 1987) showed that many parents and elementary school educators did not consider that children are really learning when they are in daycares or preschool programs. More

recently, Klein et al. (2003) also stated that the trivialization of play is still an issue today.

In their research, Egertson and Isenberg (1987) found that adults put a substantial

emphasis on academic achievement and felt that children in our society no longer needed

to play because they were too advanced for it. This notion, coupled with the emphasis on

academic achievement has helped increase the academic structure of many kindergarten

classrooms. Many early childhood educators reported that they were deeply concerned

about the developmentally inappropriate practices that were occurring in many

classrooms as parents pressured early childhood educators to prepare children for the

academic world of school (Charlesworth, Hart, & Burns, 1991).

A majority of teachers interviewed by Rothlein and Brett (1987) did not consider play

to be an "integral" component of the curriculum. They subscribed more to a "learn-play

dichotomy". The lack of importance ascribed to play was echoed in another study by

Ryn, Tagano, and Moran (2005), who found that many teachers did not feel that play was

an "appropriate" way of fostering "children's development" and supported more of an

academically structured program.

Another study (Moyer, Egertson, & Isenberg, 1987) showed that kindergarten

programs were being "misdirected". These researchers stated that this misdirection was

being caused by "societal pressure" and a lack of knowledge or misconception of

children's developmental needs. This is a sentiment that continues to be echoed today.

File and Gullo (2002) cited societal pressure on educators to teach children in

academically structured environments as a cause of concern for educators. There is also a

shortage of teachers who are trained to work specifically with young children. The problem is further compounded by marketing campaigns, which try to sell materials that are, for the most part, not suitable for young children. Due in part to the lack of qualified personnel and pressure by parents for academic structure, many kindergarten classrooms have materials that are not meeting the developmental needs of the children in those classrooms (Moyer et al., 1987). For example, a teacher who is qualified as an elementary school teacher but works with 3-and-4-year-olds is not always aware of the developmental needs of this age group and may consider materials, such as stencils and worksheets, that he/she used in their elementary school classrooms to be appropriate in an early childhood educational classroom.

The fact that many people do not seem to value play in general, and specifically in daycares and preschools, is disturbing (Rothstein & Brett, 1987). Hatch and Freeman (1988) echo this sentiment and discuss the determination of the proponents who campaign vigorously to structure kindergarten classes in a more academic manner. The advocates for developmentally appropriate practices in the early childhood classrooms have expressed concern over the fact that not much attention is paid to what young children truly need in terms of their development, "the miseducation of young children" in general and the loss of childhood that many children experience when society forces them to grow up too quickly (Hatch & Freeman, 1988). All the issues discussed in this section help make a case for the decline of play opportunities and the lack of value that our society places on play. The focus of the next section, is to discuss why play is important and how it helps children develop.

The Importance of Play for Children's Development

There are many reasons why play is important. Play has been shown to help children deal with stress, anxiety, and tension (Slavin, 1988). For example, if a new sibling has just been introduced into the family, a child can act out his or her frustration and anxiety over the event through play. A child will not be permitted to hurt the new member of the family, but can vent his/her emotions on a doll, thereby letting them release the anxiety and tension they may feel.

Play has been linked with the development of problem solving skills and creative thinking (Klein et al., 2003). Play also helps children gain an understanding of the world around them, how things work and how to use tools (Rothlien & Brett, 1987; Zeece & Graul, 1990; Klein et al., 2003). For example, by building with blocks a child develops a greater understanding of how buildings are constructed and various cognitive concepts (e.g., size, shape). When a child adds water to sand and watches the water disappear into the sand, she/he may begin to understand the process of absorption. When children dig in dirt, for example, they may learn that as the temperature becomes colder that the ground becomes harder to dig in and requires more effort.

When children play their thinking focuses on the events at hand but also extends to consider future events and the outcomes of their actions (Mellou, 1994). It is through playing that children can learn about cause and effect. They learn that their behaviour and actions have consequences. Play provides children with a natural opportunity to learn about "social rules" (Klein et al., 2003). If a child breaks something that another child has created that child will learn that it upsets others when their things are broken. The child learns the consequence that he/she should not break things that do not belong to him/her.

The definition of play and the importance of the learning process that occurs through play is further supported by Moyer et al. (1987), who discuss the many benefits of play, including the social and emotional development of children. Children also learn to think critically and solve social problems in their play (Moyer et al., 1987; Klein et al., 2003). The importance of play in aiding in children's social and emotional development has been documented more recently by Klein et al. (2003), who supported Moyer's findings. Literacy skills are also enhanced through play as children have the opportunity to interact with each other thereby developing their verbal and social skills (Klein et al., 2003). Lesseman, Rollenberg, and Rispens (2001) showed that children talk significantly more during free play time than they do during any other time in the classroom. The implication of this finding is that free play provides children with the opportunity to verbalize and socialize with each other more so than at any other period of time throughout the day, thereby helping children develop language and social skills.

Children also learn that objects can be used to represent other things. This is an important lesson that helps children understand mathematical and literacy concepts, where children must be able to grasp the concept that letters create words and words represent objects or mathematical concepts where numbers represent values.

Rothlien and Brett (1987) have also shown that play is an effective motivator for keeping children engaged in their activity, thereby helping them to increase their attention spans and also as a means to encourage children to "explore new materials and ideas". For example, if children are allowed the opportunity to play with blocks, explore them and develop their ideas they are more likely to play with the blocks for an extended period of time. More recently, Klein et al. (2003), discussed the length of time children could stay on task if they were allowed to become wholly involved in their play, a point

discussed later. Klein et al. (2003) also support the belief that children will stay on task

longer if they find an activity to be fun. This is one of the reasons why free play is

important and why the present study aims to examine teacher's attitudes towards free

play. In the next section we will look at the role of free play in a developmentally

appropriate early childhood educational center

Free Play-The Only Kind of Play

In considering the definition of play put forth by Slavin (1988) and Rubin et al.

(1983), it becomes evident that the only true form of play is free play. The definition of

free play states that children are free to choose the activity, materials and individuals with

whom they are going to play (Yang, 2000). Yang (2000) states that children who are

truly engaged in free play not only choose their activity, materials and playmates but that

they are also free to develop, stop, or change their activity as they choose. In free play,

children can develop however they want using their own ideas or those of their

classmates with whom they have chosen to engage in an activity (Yang, 2000). This

definition is further supported by other researchers (Lesseman et al., 2001), who state

that for an activity to be considered free play there is no goal, or end product that must be

met. For example, if a child chooses to play with lego and the educator instructs the child

that the lego must be used to build a house, the child is not engaged in free play. The

educator has given the child a goal to achieve and the child is no longer playing for the

sake of playing. This criterion is also included in Slavin's (1988) definition of play,

which states that play is an activity that is not goal-oriented and directed by another

person, further showing that the only true form of play is "free play".

According to Kontos and Keyes (1999), educators need to guide children's play. They state that without guidance, children between the ages of three and six, often behave impulsively and keep repeating the same play behaviours over and over again. It is important to differentiate between guiding and directing children's play. According to the constructivist philosophy, children should be allowed and encouraged to make their own decisions. Once a child has made a decision, it is the role of the teacher to guide the child in their play to help ensure that they follow through, take responsibility for their choices and to help them develop their ideas (Kontos & Keyes, 1999).

According to Yang (2000), when children are engaged in free play they often may benefit from a teacher's guidance to improve their language and problem solving skills. Free play, in particular, is important because it allows children the opportunity to develop their decision making skills, explore different activities and materials, find out what their personal likes and dislikes are, and learn that choices have consequences (Yang, 2000).

Children do not only engage in play for the moment; they develop their critical thinking skills; absorbing and storing information for future use (Yang, 2000). For example if a child is painting and makes a hole in the paper by putting an excessive amount of paint in one particular spot, with the teacher's guidance, the child can understand why the paper tore. This information will be incorporated into the child's thinking and may be recalled the next time the child paints.

Free play also gives children a sense of power (Zeece & Graul, 1990). Children live in a world that is predominantly controlled by adults. When a child is given the opportunity to choose what he/she wants to do and then learns to manipulate materials and toys in a manner that has a positive outcome, and helps foster a positive self-image

(Zeece & Graul, 1990). Free play periods allow educators the chance to guide children to think and choose activities that are meaningful to them and help them reflect on their choices (Yang, 2000). For free play to be a positive and valuable experience for children it is important that educators guide children and ensure that they consider their choices and follow through on them. Without follow through and guidance, free play can evolve into a chaotic environment (Yang, 2000) which may be a negative experience for children and teachers alike.

Many teachers and parents dislike the concept of free play because many see it as chaotic; a time when children run wild, doing whatever they want, with whomever they want. We must be careful, however, when we define an environment as "chaotic". There is a misconception, according to researchers (Hyang-Ryn et al., 2005) that schools are meant to teach, and the way to do this is with structure and discipline. An environment without academic structure, that appears to be chaotic and undisciplined, is not considered to be an effective learning environment (Hyang-Ryn et al., 2005). Miller (1989) argued that when children are in environments where there is much focus placed on order and neatness, they may become inhibited. It is very difficult for the creative juices to flow if a child must worry about making a mess.

The difficulty with free play is that it can become a free-for-all where children are active and aimless (Stollar & Dye Collins, 1994). This behaviour only occurs if a teacher allows it to happen and does not set limits regarding respectful behaviour. Teachers must guide children and support them in their play. If children are allowed to jump from one activity to another and are not asked to take some responsibility for their actions the result can be that children's opportunities for learning and development is substantially reduced. This is not to say that children should not be allowed to change their activity. As Stoller and Dye-Collins (1994) point out, it is normal for children to want to experiment and explore different areas. Children are naturally curious and we, as teachers, want to encourage that curiosity and excitement for exploring. The problem arises when children change activities with extreme frequency, are unable to stay on task for any length of time, and when teachers do not guide or support children in their play so as to encourage longer and more intensive investigation (Stoller & Dye-Collins, 1994). Teachers may support, or guide, children's play by asking them open-ended questions, offering materials to extend or develop the children's play, and creating a classroom atmosphere in which children feel comfortable and secure.

When a teacher is involved in an activity it encourages the children to participate in the activity (Kontos, 1999). While children will play on their own without adult involvement, the quality of their play may be of a higher level if an adult participates (Zeece & Graul, 1990). Rothstein and Brett (1987) found that when teachers became involved in the sociodramatic play of children that the level of play increased. If an adult understands that children learn through play they can help the child develop their play by fostering an environment that enhances and takes children's play to a higher level (Zeece & Graul, 1990). In conclusion, educators need to become involved, to become active participants but not take over control of the play, to ask questions, to observe and to structure the environment and the time continuum so as to help children reap the most benefits from their play experiences (Rothlein & Brett, 1987). The subject of time will now be discussed in the next section, which looks at both the amount of time educators spend with children and the effects the duration of play periods has on children's play.

Free Play and Time

Kontos (1999) demonstrated that while teachers do spend a substantial amount of their time interacting with children in their classrooms, they spend an inconsequential amount of time interacting one-on-one with the individual children because of the ratios and other tasks that teachers must accomplish during their day. Leseman et al. (2001) have shown that when children engage in free play with a minimal amount of input from educators, this has an impact on their behaviour. For example, aggressive children were more aggressive, and children who had difficulty staying on-task demonstrated more difficulty staying focused when teachers interacted less with them. Smilansky and Shefatya (1990) reported that children from lower socioeconomic backgrounds tended to focus their play more on the toys than on their peers. By taking time to interact and guide these children, teachers can facilitate their level of play with their peers.

Teachers spend significantly more time interacting with children during "work time" in comparison to the amount of time that they spend interacting with children during free play time (Leseman et al., 2001). The quality of the interaction was also of a lower quality during free play time. Many of the teachers' verbalizations were related to giving instructions or were not related to the play (Leseman et al., 2001).

It has been found that the amount of time children are given to play has a large impact on the type of play that they engage in with others. Researchers (Mellou, 1994) found that children who were given 30 minutes of play time had far more complex and richer play than those who only had 15-minute play periods. Young children need some time to organize and start their play. Without adequate time children are not able to develop and complete their play in a natural and appropriate manner (Zeece & Graul,

1990). It has been suggested that children of preschool and kindergarten age would benefit from having two short play periods combined into one longer play period (Christie, Johnsen, & Peckover, 1988). These authors state that having one extended play period would allow children the necessary time to develop their play into higher, more complex forms.

In conclusion, although authors have written about the importance of free play, the arguments are not based on empirical studies but more on "expert opinions", qualitative studies and teacher's opinions. There is a need for empirical research, and this is why the research being put forth in this study is valuable.

Having looked at the definition of play, the problems facing play, factors that impact children's play, and the importance of play and free play in particular, the next section of this thesis will now discuss the role of the teacher and the classroom environment in a developmentally appropriate free play period.

Methodology of Free Play

Research has shown, and continues to show that there is a correlation between social, emotional, cognitive, and academic development of children and the teachers' behaviour (Moulton et al., 1999). Moulton et al. (1999) discussed the relation between different teaching styles and child outcomes thus, suggesting that while it is important for teachers to maintain order in their classrooms to help facilitate children's development, authoritarian teachers who maintain rigid control and have tightly structured classes will not have environments that provide children with the highest levels of learning experiences. Howes and Smith (1995) demonstrated that teachers who interact in a positive manner with their students have classes in which the children feel securely attached to their teachers. It stands to reason that there would be a correlation between children feeling emotionally secure and being in an environment where they feel cared about and are made to feel important. Howes and Smith (1995) showed that children were more emotionally secure with teachers engaged in positive social interaction. Further, there was a positive association between teachers who offered more creative play activities, whether or not they engaged in positive social interaction with the children, and cognitive activity in children (Howes & Smith; 1995). Either way teachers have an important impact on children and an important element of any classroom is that a teacher should create an environment in which students feel that they are psychologically safe (Tagano, Sawyers, & Moran, 1989). By providing support for children in their play, by observing and assisting them in negotiating and helping guide children to solve their own problems, educators assist children to become independent and confident at solving their own problems (Klein et al., 2003).

Successful teachers, according to Moulton et al. (1999) are those who offer their students a wide range of activities, encourage children to be independent while at the same time interacting with them. These findings supports other researchers (Howes & Smith, 1995), who state that good teachers keep criticism and negative comments to a bare minimum while having a high level of positive verbal interaction with the children. Moulton's (1999) research shows that teachers who created the environment of their classrooms based on these criteria had students who were more spontaneous, creative, sympathetic, demonstrated high levels of task involvement, language comprehension, and participated more in the social aspects of the classroom. In classrooms with positive environments children were less dominating and hostile towards one another.

Thus, teachers create a "positive environment in their classroom by being flexible, warm, responsive, compassionate, showing interest in the children by participating in their activities, being aware of their progress and encouraging spontaneity and creativity" (Yardley, 1971 in Moulton et al., 1999, p. 21). A good teacher asks many open-ended questions and gives children time to think and form their own ideas. Teachers should also incorporate the interests of the individual children into the activities that they offer the children (Tagano et al., 1989). Teachers should encourage children to solve their own problems by giving them extended play periods. Longer play periods also allow children the time that they need to truly develop and become involved in their play as was discussed earlier. By offering children adequate time to explore an activity, teachers are helping students develop their creativity. Children should be permitted to leave an activity or project and come back to it for days or weeks at a time (Tagano et al., 1989).

Both theory (as discussed in a later section) and research have suggested a positive correlation between the level of children's competence and their interaction with adults who help guide the children by engaging in dialogue that helps children develop their language and their play (Kontos & Keyes, 1999). Research has also found that there is a correlation between the number of times children interact with an adult who is positive and/or responsive and the level of competence children display when interacting with their peers and materials (Kontos & Keyes, 1999).

There is a link between the teacher's attitude towards play and that of the children's attitude towards the subject (Mellou, 1994). If a teacher does not seem interested in what the children are doing and fails to interact, or engage in the children's play, they are less likely to persevere and focus on their activity at hand. The children almost seem to mirror the attitude of the teacher. If the teacher fails to validate their play by being enthusiastic about what the children are doing then the message that the children receive is that play is not something worth spending their time doing (Mellou, 1994). In contrast, if a teacher is excited and interested in children's play, the children will mirror the enthusiasm and interest of the teacher (Mellou, 1994).

One point that is consistently raised in the literature, is what is the role of an educator during play time? The point that appears to be so important, in a developmentally appropriate program, is the notion of the educator as a guide or a facilitator of children's play. This is an idea that was developed by Vygotsky, who will be discussed in a later section of this proposal. The role of educator as a guide is one of the key components of the constructivist philosophy. Due to children's limited life experiences they are only capable of taking their play so far and at a certain point their play stagnates (Mellou, 1994). The role of the teacher is to guide the children and to scaffold their play to the next level. While guiding the children's play teachers must be careful that they do not impose their ideas on the children's play but rather help the children develop their own ideas, thereby fostering the children's own creativity and imagination. This perspective is further supported by Ryn et al. (2005), who stated that teachers should actively involve themselves in the children's play in such a way as to take it to a higher level.

In talking to children, teachers need to ensure that they are not imposing their perspective on the child's play but are helping the child develop his/her own ideas. For example, if a teacher suggests playing with farm animals in the barn because she/he associates the animals and the barn together she/he is essentially imposing her perspective on the child. By posing an open-ended question such as, "Can you think of anything you would like to put in the barn?" or "Where can you play with the animals?" the teacher is leaving the play open to the child's will and direction. In essence, teachers engaging in developmentally appropriate practices ensure that they are creating a child-centred free play experience rather than a teacher-centred one. Smilansky and Shefatya (1990) have shown that the level of children's play shows a significant increase when adults become involved and interact with children. Smilansky and Shefatya (1990) also stressed the importance of ensuring that when educators guide, or intervene, in children's play that they focus their intervention on the skill and not the content of the play. It is important for teachers to maintain a skill-centred focus because they do not want to influence the content, or creative aspect of children's play (Smilansky & Shefatya, 1990). For example, it would be appropriate for an educator to help a child to tie a piece of string to a plastic tree to make a place for a monkey to swing. It would be inappropriate for a teacher to tell a child that they should do this, as this would be impacting on the content of their play and changing the play from child-initiated to teacher-directed.

In sum, educators may use a variety of tools to guide children's play. By observing the children, the materials they use, and the roles they take on in their play, as well as by posing direct and/or open ended questions educators can help children take their play to a higher level (Smilansky & Shefatya, 1990).

The Developmentally Appropriate Classroom

The National Association of Educators of Young Children (NAEYC) believes that it is crucial that early childhood educators provide children with the opportunity to engage in child-centred learning. It is the NAEYC position that children should be involved to some degree in deciding on the curriculum that they are going to study (Vartulli, 1999).

While the NAEYC recognizes that educators have to adapt their teaching methods to the various cognitive and social abilities of older and younger children, the position is that it is crucial that children always be permitted to be involved at some level in deciding on what goes on in their classroom and always be given responsibility for their own learning, regardless of their age (Vartulli, 1999). Other researchers (Zeece & Graul, 1990) support this position and cite the importance of children being given the chance to make their own decisions and the opportunity to engage in activities that promote development social, and cognitive development. Kontos (1999) and Leseman et al. (2001) also stress the importance of providing children with open-ended forms of play to aid in their cognitive development.

It has been demonstrated that children who attend high quality early childhood programs attain substantial benefits (Barclay & Benelli, 1995/96) and one of the most important aspects of a good program is the interaction between teachers and children (Kontos, 1999). The position statement put forth by NAEYC echoes the importance of a positive teacher-child relationship as being critical to a developmentally appropriate classroom (Vartulli, 1999). Zeece and Graul (1990) argue that how the time continuum is broken up in the classroom and the behavioural expectations of children and teachers as more important than the physical components of the classroom.

The number of children in a class is another important element to consider. Educators of large groups of children are found to engage in more developmentally inappropriate practices than educators with fewer children in their classes (Buchanan et al., 1998). The number of children in a class affects the amount of individual attention educators can give to children and may also affect the amount of time children must wait to use

materials.

A high quality early childhood educational program is also marked by an air of respect

that extends between all participants (Baclay & Benelli, 19995/96). For example, parents

should be encouraged to participate in the program and children should be talked to in

such as way as to encourage them to express their ideas and needs openly. A classroom

that is developmentally appropriate will be structured more around center or group based

activities (Burt, et al. 1992). Specifically, the activities offered in a developmentally

appropriate class are concrete, thus the children have the opportunity to touch, manipulate

and interact with materials. By creating an environment where children can explore,

manipulate, test and play, educators are providing children with the opportunity to

become excited about learning. This is crucial if early childhood educators are to be able

to help children develop the idea that learning is fun (Klein et al., 2003). While educators

in a developmentally appropriate classroom will plan group based activities, the children

will not be forced to participate in them, as they often would in a developmentally

inappropriate classroom setting. Educators will plan transitional activities (e.g., looking

at storybooks, playing with kaleidoscopes) and workbooks would never be used in a high

quality educational program (Burts et al., 1992).

Burt et al. (1992) found that children in kindergarten classes with developmentally

inappropriate practices had significantly higher stress levels than children in

developmentally appropriate classes. They also found that preschool children who

attended preschools that focused on academics and did not engage in developmentally

appropriate practices had more negative attitudes towards school than children who attended preschools that used developmentally appropriate practices. The children in the highly academically structured preschools were also found to be less creative and did not perform as well socially as their preschool counterparts who attended the developmentally appropriate preschools (Burt et al., 1992). The term developmentally appropriate practice, is a recurring one and is often linked with concepts associated with the constructivist philosophy.

Having examined the definition of play, the importance of play, and the role of the educator and environment, we will now discuss the beliefs and practices of teachers and the impact they have on teachers' classroom practices.

Educator's Beliefs and Practices

It is important to examine the attitudes and beliefs of educators as it helps us to understand and explain the varying teaching practices of educators (Isenberg, 1990). Education and beliefs are two of the strongest variables that influence observable teaching practices (Maxwell et al., 2001). Even when educators report sharing similar beliefs they often implement them into their teaching strategies in different ways.

Preschool teachers in one study (Spodek, 1988 in Charlesworth et al., 1991) showed that when questioned about their teaching practices most early childhood educators focused the majority of their attention on the management of their classrooms and the planning and organizing of activities. The topics of developmental needs of children, play, and learning were given an insignificant amount of attention. Preschool teachers paid more attention to the subject of play than kindergarten teachers who focused more on the evaluation of students. Charlesworth et al. (1991) also discussed the results of research showing that if educators are not provided with a good solid theoretical guide with detailed classroom practices to follow their practices were unlikely to follow their beliefs. Interestingly the correlation between educators who have inappropriate beliefs and engage in more developmentally inappropriate practices is slightly stronger than the correlation between educators believing in and implementing developmentally appropriate practices. Furthermore, many early childhood educators who were interviewed expressed their beliefs in vague terms rather than supporting specific theoretical beliefs (Charlesworth et al., 1991). Maxwell et al. (2001) also state that the strength in the beliefs put forth by educators is significantly higher than their level of implementation of their beliefs.

Charlesworth et al. (1991) noted that kindergarten teachers would offer developmentally appropriate activities. The activities, however, were often used as a reward for when children had finished their work. Children who took too long to complete their work were, therefore, not given the opportunity to play.

The educational background of teachers impacts on their teaching practices. Teachers who major in early childhood education have stronger beliefs in developmentally appropriate practices than teachers who majored in elementary school education (Buchanan, Burts, Bidner, White, & Charlesworth, 1998). Kagan (1992) and Vartulli (2005) also found that student teachers were more strongly impacted by the experiences they had as student teachers than they were by the theoretical knowledge they acquired in classrooms. This finding supports the idea of how effective hands-on learning is in comparison to academically structured programs, regardless of the age of the learner (Maxwell et al., 2001). Berk (1995), in comparison, found no significant difference between the classroom behaviour of college-educated teachers and their beliefs regardless of whether or not their majors were in a child-related field. Teachers who attended

college and majored in a field unrelated to children did interact more positively with

children than teachers who had not attended college. Cassidy, Buell, Pugh-Hoese, and

Russell (1995) also found that teachers with a college education engaged in more

developmentally appropriate practices than teachers without a college education.

Berk (1995) discusses the educational background of educators in relation to their

classroom practices. She mentions that educators with training interact more, and in a

more positive way, with children than educators with no training. They use fewer

authoritarian means of controlling their classrooms and interact less often with other

adults in their classrooms. College-educated teachers engage in behaviours that

encourage the development of children's verbal skills three times as often as those

educators with only high school level education (Berk, 1995).

Berk (1991) mentions that educators who are committed to the field of early childhood

education have attitudes that are more respectful of developmentally appropriate practices

than educators who do not plan on staying in the field. Research demonstrates that more

recent graduates engage in more developmentally appropriate practices than their more

experienced, older counterparts (Maxwell et al., 2001; Vartuli, 1999). Kagan (1995) also

discusses how time and experience impact on an educator's belief system and his/her

teaching style in a positive or negative way. For example, a teacher who believes in

having a highly structured academic-style classroom will tend to believe even more

strongly in this type of practice as his/her amount of time and experience spent in the

classroom increases. In contrast, a teacher who believes in developmentally appropriate practice at the beginning of his/her career would demonstrate a strengthening of this

belief system as she/he gains experience in the classroom.

Theories of Play and Teachers' Views on how Children Learn

How and what teachers think children learn has a direct link with their teaching

practices and this has an impact on how and what students learn (Vartulli, 1999; Kagan &

Smith, 1988). According to the attribution theory, if an educator believes that children

learn most effectively by rote, that teacher is most likely to have children sit and practice

repeating information until they have it memorized (Kagan & Smith, 1988). Researchers

(Buchanan, et al, 1998; Moulton, Caplan, & Mills, 1999) have shown that teacher's

attitudes impact strongly on children's experiences.

The labels continue to change but in essence the current theories and philosophies

have their roots in one of two historical camps. The first position was put forth by

Dewey, who felt that learning should be child-centred, spontaneous, and focus on the

whole child. The opposing perspective was that learning centred around developing

children's cognitive and analytical skills was more effective in children's development

(Kagan & Smith, 1988).

As discussed below Piagetian theory, which concurs with Dewey, suggests that the

most effective means of teaching children is by providing them with the opportunity to

interact spontaneously with their environment. In opposition to Piaget, is the Operant

Learning model that argues that the most effective method of imparting knowledge is to

structure specific teacher-directed learning activities for children (Kagan & Smith, 1988).

Proponents of the Operant Learning model consider the product to be of more importance

than the process. Teachers using the Operant Learning model often use extrinsic rewards such as stickers, or privileges as motivators. The Operant Learning model is based on the idea that there is one way to learn, and that the role of the teacher is to give children specific directions. Children demonstrate that they have learned by following the directions of the teacher and having an end-product to show concretely that they have learned the lesson being taught. The Operant model is not considered to be developmentally appropriate by the standards established by the National Association of Education of Young Children.

As mentioned previously, the term, developmentally appropriate practice, is often associated with the constructivist philosophy. To gain a fuller perspective, and put the constructivist philosophy in context, it is necessary to look at some of the main theories of child development and the roots of constructivism.

According to the Piagetian perspective, play basically helps children deal with the imbalance that occurs when assimilation dominates accommodation (Rubin et al., 1983). An individual who incorporates an idea into his/her existing thought pattern without changing his/her cognitive structure would be defined as assimilating the idea. The process that occurs when an idea does not fit into an individual's preexisting cognitive structure, and he/she must adapt his/her mental schema, is referred to as accommodation. For example if a child has a pet cat and then saw a small dog on the street, the child could assimilate this information and think that all animals with fur are cats. A child who was capable of accommodating this information would alter their thinking to change the characteristics of how he/she defined a cat. The behaviour that occurs as a result of this imbalance is dependent on the age and developmental level of the child. It is through play, according to Piaget, that children correct this imbalance. In the Piagetian construct a child develops a positive sense of self by repeating a behaviour, or action, until he/she

succeeds at it. It is by giving children time to rehearse a skill that they gain mastery over

it, and therefore self-confidence. According to Piaget, the first time a child engages in a

behaviour he/she is exploring and not playing. The second and recurrent times a child

engages in a behaviour he/she is playing. For example, a child who goes camping with

his/her family would not be seen to be playing camping while they were engaging in the

activity with their family. Upon returning home, however, a child who covered a table

with a blanket and crawled underneath, could be considered to be playing at camping. In

symbolic play, children use one object to represent another and/or engage in an action out

of the context in which the original activity occurred.

Piagetian theory also shares some commonalities with Freud's psychoanalytical

theory. Both theorists discuss the idea of play as a way of expressing or coping with

emotions (Rubin et al., 1983). Freud believed that play was a means for children to feel

powerful in situations where they had felt powerless. According to Freud, play is an

activity that is only engaged in for a very short time until the ego becomes more highly

developed than the id. Piaget, in comparison, believed that play continued for a much

longer period. Unlike Freud, however, Piaget did not feel that play had to necessarily

focus on emotional discord of a real-life situation but could focus on playing out the

situation to the child's desire.

Another theorist who has made a substantial contribution to the constructivist

philosophy is Vygotsky. The terms "guiding" and "scaffolding", which are often used by

constructivists and appear often in discussions about developmentally appropriate

practices, can be traced back to Vygotsky's notion of the zone of proximal development (zpd). Vygotsky believed that teachers could foster a child's cognitive development by asking questions or engaging in activities that were slightly higher than the child's current level of cognitive functioning. This slightly higher level of cognitive functioning is referred to as the zone of proximal development. He also believed that the use of objects as symbols was a critical element to childrens' play. Unlike Piaget, however, Vygotsky focused his attention on the idea that by having the capability to use one object to represent another, a child was laying the foundation to understand the concept of words representing objects. According to his theory this was the most important aspect of symbolic play.

According to Vygotsky, children should be challenged to think at a level that is slightly higher than their current level of thinking but that is attainable (Rubin et al., 1983). The role of the teacher is to observe and assess children's level of functioning and guide them to a higher level of cognition. The term, scaffolding, refers to the process of guiding a child's thinking to a higher level. Vygotsky felt that play was an effective means to create a child's zone of proximal development (Rubin et al., 1983). He wrote that to create the zpd, teachers should instruct children as to how they could solve a problem with assistance and then provide them with the opportunity to play. It was Vygotsky's belief that children who are provided with ample opportunities to socialize and play freely will become adept at solving their own problems, especially those related to socialization and communication. The constructivist idea of guiding childrens' play is related to this aspect of Vygotsky's theory.

Vygotsky felt that a key element of childrens' development was to challenge them and then to provide them with the necessary time to attain a higher level of thinking. This is another key element of developmentally appropriate practice and the constructivist philosophy.

The work of Piaget and Vygotsky represents a substantial contribution to the constructivist philosophy. Why is it that the constructivist philosophy is often discussed in relation to developmentally appropriate practices? According to Palincsar (1998), constructivism can be found to varying degrees in all the cognitive science theories. Palincsar (1998) discusses research that shows that students who are allowed to work together in an environment, where all the students are actively involved in finding solutions to specific problems, were found to have more advanced cognitive skills than their peers who worked alone. The social aspect of working together to solve problems is another element that was important in Vygotsky's theory.

The belief system of a teacher has a strong impact on their classroom practice. For example if a teacher subscribes to a cognitive development theory she/he is more likely to engage children in hands-on, active learning type of experiences. In contrast, a teacher who aligns him/herself more with the behavioral theorists is more likely to have a more academically structured classroom where he/she tells the students what to do, breaks tasks up into small steps and directs children as to how to complete them. A study by Kagan and Smith (1988) showed that educators who aligned themselves with a child-centred philosophy shared a number of common classroom practices and behaviours. The behaviours displayed by the educators in the child-centred classrooms also fit the profile of an effective early childhood educator, which is:

An early childhood teacher encourages independent activity, co-ordinates a number

of different activities simultaneously, does not overtly direct children and maintains a high level of verbal interaction with students (Kagan & Smith, 1988).

Maxwell, McWilliam, Hemmeter, Jones Ault, and Schuster (2001) discuss the

characteristics of a developmentally appropriate teacher. In their study, they state that

educators should make decisions related to their classroom practices based on a solid

understanding of child development, the needs and interests of all the children in their

class as well as being sensitive to the social and cultural backgrounds of the individual

children. Maxwell et al. (2001) also state that many of the ideas of developmentally

appropriate practices are based in the works of Piaget and Vgotsky and acknowledge the

constructivist philosophy as being developmentally appropriate. Teachers' beliefs and

how they impact on children's play opportunities is the second area of interest in the

current proposal.

The Present Study

After reviewing the literature carefully, it is apparent that the subject of play is one

that is truly valuable and well worth studying. The literature reports that children make

significant developmental gains when they are provided with the opportunity to play.

The definitions put forth also demonstrate that the only true form of play is that of free

play and that educators play a crucial role by guiding and scaffolding children's play to

higher levels. When examining the various educational philosophies, it became apparent

that the constructivist philosophy places significant value on the importance of free play,

whereas other philosophies (e.g., Montessori, directed learning) place less emphasis on

free play. The study being put forth in this proposal is to investigate educators' attitudes

towards free play and how those attitudes impact on children's free play opportunities.

The method of study will include observing the teachers in their classrooms for two 30-

minute periods of free play on two separate occasions. The teacher's behaviours will be measured using the Teaching Practice Observation Scale. Prior to the observations, the classrooms will be rated according to the Early Childhood Environment Rating Scale. After the first observation each teacher will be individually interviewed, and tape recorded by the researcher about her attitudes and beliefs towards play.

Three hypotheses are proposed by this study. The first hypothesis is that educators with higher levels of education will interact in a more developmentally appropriate manner with children than educators with lower levels of education. This hypothesis is based on the findings of Cassidy et al. (1995), Berk (1995), and Buchanan et al. (1998), who demonstrated an association between higher levels of education and increased usage of developmentally appropriate teaching practices. Developmentally appropriate teaching based on observations of developmentally appropriate practices will be demonstrated by educators engaging in frequent positive interaction with all children. Positive interaction would include, but not be limited to, such behaviours as smiling, using a warm, friendly tone of voice, asking open-ended questions, encouraging children, and talking to children at their eye-level.

The second hypothesis is that educators who subscribe to the constructivist philosophy will engage in more developmentally appropriate interaction with children than educators who believe in more instructivist philosophies. A constructivist philosophy will be identified by teachers' references to developmentally appropriate practices during the interview session, for example discussing the importance of guiding children's play or the provision of open-ended activities. The associations between a constructivist philosophy and the teacher's ECERS scores for Activities and Language will be examined.

The third, and final, hypothesis is that teachers who believe that free play is important will provide more free play opportunities for children than teachers who do not value free play. For example, teachers who believe in the value of free play will provide children with longer periods of free play and fewer teacher-structured activities than teachers who do not place a significant value on the importance of free play opportunities to children's development.

Method

Participants

For the study a cross-section of 18 early childhood educators from 5 daycares in the Montreal area were interviewed in regards to their attitudes and beliefs in relation towards play, with a focus on free play, and the role of the teacher. The directors of 8 centers (see Appendix A) were contacted and the purpose of the study was explained. After speaking with the directors, and obtaining their consent (see Appendix B), meetings will be arranged with English speaking educators of the 3-and 4-year-old children to explain the purpose of the study. Teachers will be asked for consent (see Appendix C).

Procedures

For the purpose of this study the quality of the classrooms were assessed using the Early Childhood Environment Rating Scale (see Appendix D). The educators were each observed for 30-minute periods, on two separate occasions during their free play periods and will be rated using the Teachers' Practice Observation Scale (TPOS, see Appendix E). The educators will be privately and individually interviewed and asked a set of demographic questions. They were also asked about their classroom practices and their attitudes towards play (see Appendix F)

Measures

ECERS. The ECERS is a widely recognized rating tool used for assessing the quality of early childhood learning environments such as daycare and preschool classroom settings. The ECERS has been tested for reliability and validity on numerous occasions (Cassidy et al. 1995) and provides an overview of all aspects of an early childhood educational program (Barclay & Bernelli, 1995/96). It consists of 7 subscales: Space and Furnishings, Personal Care Routines, Language-Reasoning, Activities, Interaction, Program Structure, and Parents and Staff (see Appendix D for items). There are 43 items on the scale and each item is rated on a 7-point Likert Scale, with a score of 1 representing Inadequate and a rating of 7 being Excellent. For the purpose of the present study, only the Activities and Language subscales were used following procedures advocated by Cassidy for research purposes The ECERS was conducted before the interview sessions and it was performed by 2 researchers to establish inter-rater reliability.

Teacher's Practice Observation Scale. The educators will be observed using the Teachers Practice Observation Scale (TPOS) (Moulton, Coplan & Mills, 1999) during times of free play identified by the educators. The TPOS is a new scale, which was created by Moulton et al. (1999). The scale was designed specifically to measure teachers' behaviours during free play time. Moulton et al. (1999) reported that the overall Cohen's *kappa* of the TPOS was $K = .75$.

This scale (see Appendix E) focuses on time and behaviour management. On the TPOS scale the time management category is divided into four parts:(1) Small Group/Individual Interaction, (2) Large group interaction; (3) Ontask; and, (4) Offtask .

The second component of the codes involves looking at the ways that teachers interact with children during free play time. For this the TPOS breaks down the teacher's behaviour into seven categories (see Appendix E for definitions and examples). They are as follows:

(a) Praise and encouragement
(b) Activity participation
(c) Hostility
(d) Accepts feelings
(e) Encourages perspective taking
(f) Encourages independence

For the first and second component of the TPOS, teachers were observed for 20 seconds with a 10 second recoding period for a total of 2-30 minute time periods using an event sampling method. Specifically, the observations focused on how the teachers used his/her time (large/small group, etc.) and which of the behaviours were observed.

The third component of the TPOS focuses on the atmosphere of the classroom. There are five categories in this section, and they are as follows: (1) warmth (e.g.., how much attention and compassion does the educator demonstrate?); (2) patience (e.g., does the educator use a calm tone of voice?); (3) interest/involvement (e.g., does teacher interact with children and, ask them questions?); (4) positive affect (e.g., does teacher demonstrate physical warmth such as hugging children or smiling at them?); and, (5) time division (e.g., does teacher spend time with interacting with all members of the group?). For this aspect of the scale the educators are rated on a 3-point Likert scale every 15 minutes over the two-45 minute observation periods.

Teacher Interview. The final component of the study involved the researcher interviewing, and tape recording, each individual educator, at his/her daycare centre. Teachers were asked 37 questions related to play, specifically how he/she structures his/her individual day in his/her classroom, and some general questions related to the educator's level of education, experience in the field, and his/her personal beliefs and philosophy. Each individual interview took approximately 30-45 minutes.

Reliability

To establish inter-rater reliability, a second researcher was trained to use the TPOS Scale until the inter-rater reliability reached .70-.75. This second researcher also participated in 20-25% (n = 8/40) of the 40 teacher observations to establish inter-rater reliability. These reliability observations were evenly spaced out during the data collection.

The interview was coded using a qualitative methodology looking for themes. The results of the TPOS were also coded using a qualitative methodology, looking for behaviour that correlated with, or represented, the constructivist philosophy versus an instructivist or teacher-centred philosophy. For example does the teacher use praise and encouragement to motivate children or does he/she give many directives to children? Does he/she engage in activity with children or does he/she stand back and observe the children? The coding scheme was developed using qualitative methods for identifying themes (Strauss & Corbin, 1998).

Results

Plan of Analyses

First, the data were verified and preliminary descriptive statistics were conducted. The descriptive information about the samples is presented first, followed by the testing the three hypothesis as outlined. The analysis of the hypothesis that educators with higher levels of education would engage in more developmentally appropriate manner than educators with lower levels of education was determined by analyzing the response to question #4 of the teacher questionnaire and comparing it with the ECERS Scores in the #16 item of the Language Reasoning section and, the Activities, Interaction and Program Structure subscales. The teacher's responses to question #4 were also analyzed in relation to the TPOS scale and the teacher's responses to questions 6-37 of the questionnaire. Correlations were used to analyze this question.

The first hypothesis that teachers who had higher levels of education would engage in more developmentally appropriate practices was analyzed by comparing teacher's responses to the Interview Questions relating to their levels of education with the ECERS Language and Activity codes. The Interview Question responses were also analyzed for correlations with the TPOS scores.

The second hypothesis that educators who subscribed to the constructivist philosophy would engage in more developmentally appropriate interaction than educators who believed in other philosophies was analyzed by examining teacher's responses to the questions related to their beliefs and practices with the ECERS Activities, Interaction and, Program Structure subscales and, the TPOS Scale results. Again, correlations were used to analyze this question.

The third hypothesis that educators who believed in the value of free play would provide children with longer periods of free play and fewer teacher-structured activities than teachers who did not place a significant value on the importance of free play

opportunities to children's development was determined by analyzing teacher's responses

to the questions relating to the amount of time he/she allocated for free play/structured

time, the ECERS Program Structure subscale and the TPOS Scale results. The teacher's

responses were reviewed to determine if there was a correlation between their responses

to the questions and the results of the ECERS and the TPOS Scale.

Following the hypothesis testing a series of exploratory analyses were conducted.

The first analyses focused on the association between the ECERS and the TPOS

measures. First, the ECERS Activities scores and TPOS teacher behaviours were

analyzed. Second, the ECERS Language scores and TPOS teacher behaviour was

discussed. Third, the associations between ECERS Activity codes and TPOS teacher

activity codes were reviewed. Next the association between the ECERS Activity codes

and the TPOS emotional climate classroom were analyzed. The last measure that was

analyzed was the Teacher Interview questionnaire. The first components that were

reviewed were all the interview responses related to free play and structured time in the

classrooms. Finally, associations between the ECERS and the Interview Questionnaire

responses were completed, specifically the intercorrelations between the ECERS Total

Language and Activity codes and Interview Questionnaire responses and then the

Interview Questionnaire responses were correlated with the TPOS scores.

Preliminary Data Considerations and Descriptive Statistics

The first step was to check and verify the data scoring and entry. Next, the internal

consistency of the ECERS was determined by the use of the *alpha* coefficient. The

Cronbach's *alpha* for the Activities subscale (12 items) = .71, for the Language subscale

(9 items) = .72 and for the Total Score (Activities plus Language subscales) = .73. The three *alphas* were considered acceptable indicators of the internal consistency of the scales. __

The means, standard deviations, and ranges for the items on the ECERS are found in Table 1 (all tables are found at the end of the Results section). The means for the individual items and participating centres were all relatively high. This could be due to the fact that the centres which chose to participate were all affiliated with a college early childhood education program and, were therefore likely of a higher standard than the average childcare centre. The areas in which the means were the lowest were *space for privacy, nature/science* and *promoting acceptance of diversity*.

The descriptive statistics for the TPOS measure and the teacher interviews are found in Table 2. The individual scores for the ECERS and TPOS can be found in Appendix C and H respectively.

Hypothesis One Findings

There were no significant correlations found in relation to hypothesis one, that teachers with higher levels of education would engage in more developmentally appropriate practices than teachers with lower levels of education. This could be due to the small sample size and the fact that there was not a wide distribution in the levels of education of the teachers participating in the study.

Hypothesis Two Findings

In relation to hypothesis two, that teachers who subscribed to a constructivst philosophy would engage in more developmentally appropriate practices than teachers who followed more of an instructivist approach; no significant associations were found.

Again, this could be due to the small sample size and the fact that there was not a significant variance in any of their philosophical approaches..

Hypothesis Three Findings.

In relation to hypothesis three, that teachers who believed in the value of free play would provide longer periods of free play and have less teacher-structured activities, there were no significant associations. This could be due to the small sample size and the fact that all the teachers believed in the value of free play and therefore there was no variance in the scores.

Given that the hypotheses were not supported a series of more detailed exploratory analyses of the data were conducted. The internal consistency of each measure was explored as well as associations between measures.

ECERS: Measure of Classroom Quality.

The general purpose of these analyses was first to examine the intracorrelations between items on the Activities and Language Subscales and second, to investigate the intercorrelations between the two subscales.

Activities subscale intracorrelations. The purpose of these analyses was to look at the relationship between the items on the ECERS Activities subscale (see Table 3). A number of significant positive correlations were evident. Furniture for relaxation and comfort (item 3) was significantly correlated with art (20) blocks (22), dramatic play (24). Books and pictures (item 15) demonstrated a significant positive correlation with blocks (22), sand (23), and math (26). Fine motor (item 19) was positively correlated with sand (23) and dramatic play (24). Art (item 20) was positively associated with blocks (22). Music/movement (item 21) was found to have a significant negative correlation with nature (25) and a highly significant positive correlation with promoting

diversity (28). Blocks (item 22) demonstrated a highly significant correlation with sand

(23) and dramatic play (24). Sand/water (item 23) demonstrated a significant positive

correlation with dramatic play (24) and with math/number (26). Finally nature/science

(item 25) was positively associated with math (26). In conclusion, the intracorrelations

demonstrate a high degree of correlation between items and support the high *alpha*,

which indicates high internal consistency of the subscale items.

Language subscale intracorrelations. The purpose of these analyses was to examine

the associations between the scores on the language subscale (see Table 4). It was not

possible to correlate the scores for *Greeting/departing, Staff-child interaction* and

Interaction among the children as there was no variability in their scores. All centers

received a score of seven for all three items.

Encouraging children to communicate (item 16) was found to have a correlation with

general supervision of children (30) and with group-time (36). Using language to

develop reasoning skills (item 17) had a significant correlation with informal use of

language (18) and with general supervision of children (30). Informal use of language

(item 18) had a significant positive correlation with using language to develop reasoning

skills (17) and with general supervision of children (30). General supervision of children

(item 30) demonstrated a positive correlation with encouraging children to communicate

(16), using language to develop reasoning skills (17), with informal use of language (18)

and discipline (31). Discipline (item 31) also had a positive correlation with group-time

(36). Group-time (item 36) demonstrated a highly significant positive correlation with

encouraging children to communicate (16) and discipline (31). In conclusion, these analyses demonstrate that teachers who are involved and communicate effectively with children do encourage language development and reasoning skills. The intracorrelations indicate a high degree of correlation between items and support the high *alpha* reported earlier.

Intercorrelations of Activities and Language subscales. The purpose of these analyses was to examine the relationship between the Language and Activity items (see Table 5). There were only five significant correlations. Encouraging children to communicate (item 16) was positively correlated with music/movement (21). General supervision of children (item 30) was negatively associated with books (15) and positively associated with promoting acceptance of diversity (28). Discipline (item 31) and music/movement (21) were also positively correlated. A highly significant positive correlation was found between group-time (item 36) and music/movement (21). These findings suggest that the two subscales were generally measuring independent and not overlapping constructs.

Finally, the two subscales were also highly correlated with the Total ECERS (see Table 5a), namely (Activities and Total score, $r = .85$, $p <. 05$); Language and Total Score, $r = .65$, $p < .05$). However, the Activities and Language Subscales were not significantly correlated ($r = .22$, *ns*) indicating they measured independent constructs.

TPOS Measure of Teacher Behaviour

The TPOS measure assessed (1) teacher's contact with children, (2) teacher's behaviour addressed to the children and (3) the emotional climate of the classroom. Analyses are reported first for the teacher's behaviour, second for the teacher's contact with children and, thirdly for the emotional climate of the classroom.

Intracorrelations of the TPOS teacher behaviours. The purpose of these analyses was to examine the relationship between the scores of the various behaviors measured by the TPOS (see Table 6). Significant positive correlations were found between teachers' praising children (item 6) with their activity participation (8) and between teacher's addressing children's behavior (9) and addressing personality issues (10). Correlations were found between teachers' addressing personality (item 10) and encouraging perspective taking (13).

Intracorrelations of TPOS activity codes. The purpose of these analyses was to assess the associations between the items (see Table 7). A significant negative correlation was found between teachers who interacted with a small group of children (item 1) and a large group of children (2). Teachers being observed without children but on-task (item 3) also demonstrated a highly significant negative correlation with teachers being without children and off-task (4). Finally, a positive correlation was found between teachers being without children and on-task (item 4) and without children and off-task (5).

Intracorrelations of TPOS emotional climate codes. Next, the associations between teachers' behaviour and the emotional climate of the classroom were reviewed (see Table 8). Correlations were found between a positive emotional climate of the classrooms (item 1) with teachers who were interested and involved with the children (3) and who were patient (4). A cluster of highly significant positive correlations was found between teachers who were warm and responsive (2) with teachers that were interested and involved with children (3), teachers who were patient (4), and who displayed positive affect towards the children (5). Significant correlations were also found between teachers who were interested and involved with children (item 3) and who were patient (4) and who demonstrated a positive affect (5). Teachers' patience levels (4) were also found to be positively correlated with teachers who demonstrated positive affect (5).

Associations between teacher behaviours and activity codes. The purpose of the next set of analyses (see Table 9) was to examine the correlations between the teacher behaviours and the teacher activity behaviour (i.e., group size). Significantly negative correlations were found between praise (item 6) and teachers' who were without children (3). Negative correlations were also found between teachers who participated in an activity (item 8) and being without children (3) and being without children but on-task (4). Teachers who addressed behaviour issues (item 9) were also less likely to be without children and off-task (5). Negative correlations were found between teacher's who addressed children's personality (item 10) and small group size (1) and teacher's being without children and on-task (4) and without children and off-task (5). Addressing personality issues (item 10) was also positively associated with large group activity (2).

Associations between teacher behaviours and emotional climate. The purpose of the next set of analyses was to examine the association of teachers' behaviours and the emotional climate of the classroom (see Table 10). A positive correlation was found between praise (item 6) and teachers being interested and involved with children (3). Negative correlations were found between hostility (item 7) and teachers who were warm and responsive (2) and who demonstrated positive affect (5). Activity participation (item 8) was positively correlated with teachers being interested and involved with children (3). Teacher's acceptance of children's feelings (item 11) and dividing time equally amongst children (6) were also positively correlated. Finally, another positive correlation existed between teachers who encouraged children's independence (item 13) and a positive

emotional climate (1) in the classroom

Associations between TPOS activity codes and emotional climate. The purpose of the

next set of analyses was to examine the associations between the teacher's activity and

the emotional climate of the classroom. A significant negative correlation was found (see

Table 11) between teachers being without the children (item 3) and teachers being

interested and involved with the children (3). Teachers being without children and on-

task (item 4) was negatively correlated with the emotional climate of the classroom (1).

The total TPOS scores were calculated by summing the scores for each of the

categories of the two-15 minute observations for each of the two-30 minute observations.

The total scores can be found on Table 5a.

Associations between the ECERS and TPOS Measures

The purpose of these exploratory analyses was to investigate the relationship between

the quality of communication and activities of the classrooms as measured by the ECERS

and the teacher behaviour and emotional climate of the classrooms, as measured by the

TPOS.

ECERS Activities and TPOS teacher behaviours. The purpose of this analysis was to

examine the relationship between the ECERS Activities scores with the TPOS teacher

behaviour codes (see Table 12). In this analysis a highly significant correlation was

found between space for privacy (item 5) and teacher's who demonstrated hostility (7).

Significant negative correlations were also found between books/pictures (item 15) and

teacher's who addressed behaviour (9) and addressed personality issues (10). Fine motor activities (item 19) were positively correlated with teachers offering children praise (item 6). Finally nature/science (item 25) was negatively correlated with hostility (item 7).

ECERS Language and TPOS teacher behaviour. The purpose of these analyses was to examine the relationship between teachers' language and their behaviour with children (see Table 13). Encouraging children to communicate (item 16) demonstrated a significant positive correlation with praise (6). There was a cluster of correlations between teachers who accepted children's feelings (item 11) and encouraging children to communicate (16), using language to develop reasoning skills (17), informal use of language (18), and general supervision of children (30). General supervision of children (item 30) was also correlated with teacher's use of praise (6) and encouraging perspective taking (12).

Associations between ECERS Activity codes and TPOS teacher activity codes. The purpose of these analyses was to examine the relationship between the activities offered in the classroom with the teachers' behavior in regard to variables such as group-size (see Table 14). Dramatic play (item 24) was negatively correlated with teachers being without children (3). Nature/science (item 25) was found to be correlated with teachers being without children and off-task (5). There were no significant correlations found between the total ECERS activity scores and the TPOS teacher activity codes.

Associations between ECERS Language codes and TPOS teacher activity codes. The purpose of these analyses was to examine the relationship between teachers' language and the size of the group of children she/he was interacting with (see Table 15). A significant positive correlation was found between books and pictures (item 15) and teachers being without children but on-task (item 4) and being without children and off-task (5). A significant positive correlation was found between small group size (item 1) and discipline (31). There were no significant correlations found between any of the total ECERS Language scores with the TPOS teacher activity codes.

Associations between ECERS Activity items and TPOS emotional climate. The purpose of these analyses was to examine the relationship between the scores of the ECERS activity with the emotional climate found in the classroom (see Table 16). In relation to the Activities component, dramatic play (item 24) was the only activity which demonstrated a significant correlation with teachers being interested and involved with children's play (3) and with teachers who exhibited patience (4) with children. There were no significant correlations found between any of the total ECERS Activity scores with the emotional climate of the classroom.

Intercorrelations between ECERS Language codes and TPOS emotional classroom climate The purpose of these analyses was to explore the relationship between the ECERS language items and the emotional climate (see Table 17). In terms of the language component, there was a cluster of correlations between teachers who encouraged children to communicate (item 16) and being warm and responsive (2), being interested and involved with children (3), teachers who demonstrating patience (4), and displayed positive affect (5). Using language to develop reasoning skills (item 17) was positively correlated with teachers displaying positive affect (5) and dividing time equally amongst children (6). Informal use of language (item 18) was positively correlated with teachers who were interested and involved with children (3), displaying positive affect (5) and with teachers who divided time equally amongst all the children (6). General supervision of children (item 30) was positively correlated with teachers who were interested and involved with the children (3). Discipline (item 31) was

positively correlated with teachers who were interested and involved with the children

(3). Finally, group time (item 36) was positively associated with teachers who were

warm and responsive (2),

Teacher Interviews

Education levels and employment. The purpose of these analyses is to provide an

overview of the teachers (see Table 18). The majority of teachers reported working in the

field for over four years, but there was an equal number who had been working for

between four and six years and over ten years. None of the teachers had been working in

the field for less than a year, while 11 percent reported working for between one and

three years in early childhood education. Twenty two percent had been working for

between seven and ten years.

The most frequent level of education was attestation with 44% of respondents

reporting having attained their attestation. The second highest reported level of education

attained was the completion of a DEC, with 27% of respondents falling in this category.

The rest of the respondents, 25%, were divided evenly between having completed high

school, having completed some university undergraduate studies, completed

undergraduate studies, and having attended some graduate level courses.

The most often cited reason for working in the field of early childhood education,

given by half of respondents, was a love of children. Sixteen percent reported choosing

this field in preparation for parenthood and 11% stated that they had previously engaged

in similar work, such as babysitting or working at summer camps, and found they

enjoyed the experience. Eleven percent cited other reasons (e.g., thought the E.C.E.

program looked interesting, wanted a change of employment, 5% said it was convenient and 5% did not respond to the question.

The teachers, as a group, had a very stable level of employment. Sixty-five percent reported having been employed at their current centres for over five years. Twenty-two percent had been employed for between two and four years and sixteen percent reported having been working at their current centres for less than two years. The shortest length of employment reported was nine months and the longest was fifteen years.

Classroom play structure organization. The purpose of these analyses was to report how the educators structured, or organized their classrooms (see Table 19). A large majority of teachers, 66%, reported having between seven and eight children in their care. Thirty-three percent of respondents were evenly divided between being responsible for either nine or ten, or fourteen or sixteen children. In these cases the teachers were involved in team teaching and shared a classroom with another educator.

In terms of centre philosophy, 50% of respondents cited the centre philosophy was that of learning through play. None of the respondents were unsure of their centre's philosophy although some respondents had difficulty defining it. Twenty-seven percent of the respondents said that the philosophy involved behaviours such as being fair and encouraging autonomy. Sixteen percent defined the centre philosophy as High/Scope or Reggio Emilia. Five percent stated that it meant taking the children's interests into consideration and 11% gave other responses.

In terms of their own personal philosophies, an overwhelming majority of 55% supported a learning through play perspective. Only five percent or one individual, reported following an instructivist (e.g., teacher-centred) philosophy. Eleven percent felt that it was important to consider children's interests and levels of development while an equal number cited other considerations and children's enjoyment of the program as the basis for their personal philosophies. Only five percent of respondents were unable to state or define their personal philosophy.

Free play and structured time in the classroom. The purpose of these analyses was to report how teachers divided their time between structured activity and free play activity (see Table 20). The majority of educators (66 %) included one free play period into their classroom. Only one educator reported that they had no free play periods in their schedule and 27% of educators were at the opposite at the end of the spectrum and reported over three free play periods each day.

Fifty percent of educators stated that their free play periods were between 26-45 minutes in length. Twenty-two percent stated that their free play periods were between 45-60 minutes, with the same number reporting that their free play periods were over an hour long.

In terms of structured play periods (e.g., circle time, cooking or science activities), two educators reported having no structured play periods at all. The majority of educators (50%) reported having one structured play period during the day. One respondent did not answer and 32% were equally divided between having two or more than three structured play periods each day.

In terms of the amount of time devoted to the structured activities, 16% reported that their structured play periods were less than fifteen minutes in length. One educator stated that her structured play period continued for more than sixty minutes. Twenty-two percent reported children engaged in structured play for between 45-60 minutes each day.

Ten educators (54%) were evenly divided between 16-25 minutes of structured play time and 25-45 minutes.

When asked about the importance of free play in their programs, 100% of the educators felt that free play was an important part of their programs and gave it equal importance with structured play.

Next (question 17) educators were asked to explain their role during free play. Sixty-six percent of educators reported that their role during free play periods was to support and guide children's play. Thirty eight percent reported helping children resolve conflict and problem solve during this time. Sixteen percent used free play periods to engage in other teacher responsibilities (e.g. taking attendance, preparing crafts, putting together bulletin board display). Five percent felt that it was important to help children become more autonomous and make decisions for themselves and an equal number felt that their main role was to redirect inappropriate behavior. When asked about the importance of interacting with the children (question 18) 77% of educators agreed that it was important for educators to interact with children during free play periods, while 11% felt this was not important and five percent remained neutral on this issue. .

Question 23 asked educators to discuss what their role was during a structured activity. Sixty-six percent of educators reported providing children with materials and 50% used structured play periods to demonstrate something to children (e.g., how to make masks, how to trace and cut out paper fish, how to weave baskets with construction paper). Only five percent of educators followed the children's lead during a structured play period and another 5% engaged in some other form of behaviour during this time.

In terms of the kinds of structured activities provided to the children, arts and crafts was the most frequently reported activity, with 38% of educators reporting that this was how children spent their structured play periods. An equal number (27%) reported structuring science and games during these periods. Sixteen percent of educators stated that they set up cooking activities and 22% engaged in reading stories or other circle time activities (i.e., calendar) while another 22% of educators engaged in other forms of activities during structured play periods such as organized crafts. In terms of interacting during structured activities (Question 24), 77% of educators felt that it was important to interact with children during structured play periods. Five percent felt it was not important and another 5% stated that sometimes it was important. Eleven percent of the educators chose not to respond either because they did not have structured play time in their classroom or they could not decide whether or not it was important.

Next, question 25 focused on the educator's selection of materials for structured play periods. Seventy-two percent of educators did report preselecting materials for children to use all the time during structured activities and twenty seven percent said that sometimes they would preselect mateials. Reasons educators gave for preselecting materials included: to ensure that children played with a variety of materials; to ensure that children were playing with materials that would help meet the children's individual developmental needs; some play activities were too noisy so educators limited the time and number of children who could engage in such activities (i.e. playing with blocks, musical instruments).

Question 28 asked the educators whether they felt that structuring children's play was the best way to facilitate their learning and prepare them for school. Twenty-seven percent of the educators felt that structured play was an effective way of preparing children for school. Five percent of educators were neutral and an overwhelming 66% of educators felt that it was not a good way of preparing children for school.

The final question related to structuring children's play asked educators whether they felt that structuring children's play limited the children's creativity and hindered their ability to make choices for themselves (question 29). Seventy-seven percent of educators agreed with this statement. None of the educators remained neutral and 22% disagreed with this statement. The educators who disagreed stated that they felt that children were allowed the opportunity to make choices in other areas and that they could explore and be creative at other times..

Associations between the ECERS and the Interview Questionnaire Responses

The purpose of these analyses was to investigate hypothesis 2 regarding the relationship between the quality of communication and activities of the classrooms as measured by the ECERS and the teachers' responses to the interview questions. Specifically it was argued that teachers espousing a constructivist philosophy would score higher on the ECERS. First, the associations of the Total ECERS (Language and Activity) are reported, followed by Language and then Activities.

Intercorrelations between ECERS Total Language and Activity codes and Interview Questionnaire Responses (see Table 22). The purpose of these analyses was to explore the relationship between the total scores that teachers received on the language and activity sections of the ECERS with responses to interview questions that were of a constructivist nature. Only four significant correlations and a negative trend were found between the ECERS Language and Activity measures and the interview questionnaire responses.

A negative trend was found between teachers with high ECERS scores and teachers who stated that free play was an important aspect of their program as it contributed to a home-away-from-home type of ambience. A significant positive correlation was found between teachers who received high scores on the Language and Activity Total Scores on the ECERS and teachers who said that their role during free play was to support children's play. There was a significant negative correlation between teachers who received high Language and Activity Total scores and who felt that their role during free play was to help children become autonomous and make their own decisions. A highly significant correlation was demonstrated between high Language and Activity Total scores and teachers who stated that guiding children's play meant extending it, scaffolding or facilitating it in some manner.

Intercorrelations between ECERS Total Language Codes and Interview Questionnaire Responses (see Table 23). The purpose of these analyses was to explore the relationship between the total Language score that teachers received on the ECERS with responses to interview questions, which were of a constructivist nature.

Only two correlations and two trends were demonstrated between the ECERS Language codes and the interview questionnaire responses. A negative trend was found between teachers who received high Language scores on the ECERS with teachers who stated that free play was an important part of their program because it helped create a home-away-from-home type of atmosphere. A negative trend was also found between high ECERS Language scores and teachers who felt that free play was an important part of their program as it provided teachers with the opportunity to observe children and their

play. A significant negative correlation was demonstrated between teachers who scored

high on the ECERS Language component and teachers who stated during the interview

process that their role during free play was to help children become more autonomous

and make their own decisions. A significant positive correlation was found between

those with high Language scores and those who defined guiding children's play as

facilitating, scaffolding or extending children's play in some manner.

Intercorrelations between ECERS Total Activity Codes and Interview Questionnaire

Responses (see Table 24). The purpose of these analyses was to explore the relationship

between the total Activity score that teachers received on the ECERS with responses to

interview questions, which were of a constructivist nature.

There were only two significant correlations found between the ECERS Activity codes

and the interview questionnaire responses. A negative correlation was found between

teachers who received high ECERS Activity scores with teachers who felt that free play

was an important part of their program as it provided them with the opportunity to

observe children. The second negative correlation was demonstrated between teachers

with high Activity scores and teachers who stated that their role during free play was to

help children become more autonomous and make their own decisions.

Table 1

Means and Standard Deviations of the ECERS Variables

Items	Mean	Standard Deviation	Minimum Score	Maximum Score
Activities Subscale				
Furniture for relaxation & comfort	5.3	1.1	2	6
Space for privacy	3.6	1.3	2	7
Books and pictures	5.5	1.5	4	7
Fine motor	6.0	1.1	4	7
Art	5.8	1.3	1	6
Music/movement	4.5	1.2.	2	6
Blocks	5.4	1.0	3	6
Sand/water	6.2	1.1	4	7
Dramatic play	5.5	1.2	2	7
Nature/science	4.0	2.3	1	7
Math/number	5.2	1.0	4	7
Promoting acceptance of diversity	3.9	1.2	3	7

Total Activity Score 1105	Mean 61.38	Standard Deviation 8.13	Minimum 43.0	Maximum 74.0
Language				
Greeting/departing	7.0	0	7	7
Encouraging children to communicate	5.9	1.1	3	7
Using language to Develop reasoning skills	5.2	1.4	3	7
Informal use of language	6.0	.87	5	7
General supervision of children	6.2	1.0	4	7
Discipline	6.9	.23	6	7
Staff-child interaction	7.0	.0	7	7
Interaction among children	7.0	.0	7	7
Group-time	6.4	1.0	4	7
Total Language Score 1045	Mean 58.05	Standard Deviation 4.38	Minimum 49.0	Maximum 63.0

Table 2

Means and Standard Deviations of the TPOS Variables

Code	Mean	Standard Deviation	Minimum Scores	Maximum Scores
Time Management				
Small Group	57.6	11.7	32	81
Large Group	14.3	13.5	0	47
Without Children	16.5	8.4	3	36
On-task/Without Children	50.2	19.4	23	81
Off-task/Without Children	5.3	6.6	0	19
Teacher Behaviour Codes				
Praise/encouragement	28.5	11.4	10	50
Hostility	3.0	3.1	0	10
Activity participation	45.6	16.6	12	71
Addresses behaviour	24.3	10.6	13	50

Addresses personality	2.2	2.6	0	10
Accepts feelings	10.0	5.9	1	23
Encourages perspective taking	18.8	12.7	0	47
Encourages independence	5.2	3.6	0	12
Emotional Climate				
Noise level	10.3	1.6	6	12
Warmth/responsiveness	10.1	1.9	5	12
Interest/involvement	11.1	1.6	6	12
Patience	11.3	1.0	8	12
Positive Affect	9.4	1.8	5	12
Time Division	10.0	1.3	8	12

Table 3

Intracorrelations of ECERS Activities Scores

	(3)	(5)	(15)	(19)	(20)	(21)	(22)	(23)	(24)	(25)	(26)	(28)
(3)	--	.29	.19	.25	.50*	.25	.60**	.32	.66**	-.06	-.03	-.02
(5)		--	.17	.03	.19	.25	.02	-.05	.03	-.43	.06	.09
(15)			--	.38	.28	-.08	.52*	,65**	.42	.31	.69**	-.04
(19)				--	-.07	.30	.45	.52*	.57*	.00	.09	.43
(20)					--	-.40	.47*	.25	.30	.03	.03	.37
(21)						--	.06	.21	.03	-.54*	-.03	.74**
(22)							--	.89**	.89**	.14	.43	.14
(23)								--	.71**	.05	.56*	.30
(24)									--	.31	.34	.09
(25)										--	.49*	-.29
(26)											--	-.29
(28)												--

*$p < .05$ **$p < .01$

Note. (3) = Furniture for relaxation and comfort; (5) = Space for privacy; (15) = Books and pictures; (19) = Fine motor; (20) = Art; (21) = Music/movement; (22) = Blocks; (23) = Sand/water; (24) = Dramatic play; (25) = Nature/science; (26) = Math/number; (28) = Promoting acceptance of diversity.

Table 4

Intracorrelations of ECERS Language Scores

	(9)	(16)	(17)	(18)	(30)	(31)	(32)	(33)	(36)
(9) Greeting/departing	--	--	--	--	--	--	--	--	--
(16) Encouraging children to communicate	--	--	.32	.46	.53*	.41	--	--	.80**
(17) Using language to develop reasoning skills	--	.32	--	.69**	.56*	.03	--	--	-.02
(18) Informal use of language	--	.46	.69**	--	.54*	.01	--	--	.21
(30) General supervision of children	--	.53*	.56*	.54*	--	.52*	--	--	.28
(31) Discipline	--	.41	--	--	--	--	--	--	.55*
(32) Staff-child interaction	--	--	--	-	--	--	--	--	--
(33) Interaction among children	--	--	--	--	--	--	--	--	--
(36) Group-time	--	.80**	-.02	.21	.28	.55*	--	--	--

$*p < .05$ $**p < .01$

Note. (9) = Greeting/departing; (16) = Encouraging children to communicate; (17) = Using language to develop reasoning skills; (18) = Informal use of language; (30) General supervision of children; (31) = Discipline; (32) = Staff/child interaction; (33) = Interaction among children; (36) = Group time

Table 5

Intercorrelations of ECERS Language and Activity Scores

	(3)	(5)	(15)	(19)	(20)	(21)	(22)	(23)	(24)	(25)	(26)	(28)
(9)	--	--	--	--	--	--	--	--	--	--	--	--
(16)	.22	-.12	-.04	.42	-.29	.49*	.20	.23	.40	.17	.20	.40
(17)	-.18	.04	-.08	.03	-.18	-.07	.08	-.00	.20	.40	.26	.33
(18)	-.30	-.03	-.19	.11	-.18	-.13	-.21	-.25	-.02	.39	.10	.21
(30)	.06.	.27	-.47*	.04	-.20	.39	-.06	-.16	.06	-.23	-.27	.53*
(31)	.28	.12	-.24	-.21	-.21	.49*	-.12	-.16	-.10	-.30	-.16	.18
(32)	--	--	--	--	--	--	--	--	--	--	--	--
(33)	--	--	--	--	--	--	--	--	--	--	--	--
(36)	.33	.06	.00	.31	-.25	.64**	.02	.08	.13	-.12	.13	.27

$*p < .05$ $**p < .01$

Note. (3) = Furniture for relaxation and comfort; (5) = Space for privacy; (9) = Greeting/departing; (15) = Books and pictures; (16) = Encouraging children to communicate; (17) = Using language to develop reasoning skills; (18) = Informal use of language; (19) = Fine motor; (20) = Art; (21) = Music/movement; (22) = Blocks; (23) = Sand/water; (24) = Dramatic play; (25) = Nature/science; (26) = Math/number; (28) = Promoting acceptance of diversity. (30) = General Supervision; (31) = Discipline; (32) = Staff/child interaction; (33) = Interaction among children; (36) = Group time

Table 5a

Intercorrelations between Total ECERS Activity and Language Scores with Total TPOS Scores

	(1)	(2)	(3)	(4)	(5)	(6)	(7)	(8)
Total ECERS Activity Scores (1)	--	.22	.85**	.16	.22	-.05	-.00	.25
Total ECERS Language Scores (2)		--	.65**	.45	-.28	.29	-.06	.65**
Total ECERS Language & Activity Scores (3)			--	.38	-.01	.10	.00	.52*
Total time teacher With children (4)				--	-.59**	.67**	.25	.24
Total time teacher Without children (5)					--	-.62**	.05	-.37
Total teacher negative behaviour (6)						--	.03	.25
Total teacher positive Behaviour (7)							--	-.41
Total emotional climate Of classroom (8)								--

$*p < .05 **p < .01$

Table 6

TPOS Intracorrelations of Teacher Behaviour Codes

	(6) Praise	(7) Hostil.	(8) Activ. Partic.	(9) Address Behaviour.	(10) Address. Person	(11) Acc. Feel	(12) Enc. p/tak	(13) Enc. ind.
(6) praise	--	.02	.54*	.11	.40	.28	.29	.06
(7) hostility		--	-.40	.46	.14	.04	.46	.16
(8) activity participation			--	.01	.43	-.19	-.04	.15
(9) addresses behaviour				--	.78**	.19	.45	.16
(10) addresses personality					--	.26	.56*	.31
(11) accepts feelings						--	.35	.43
(12) encourages perspective							--	.39
(13) encourages independence								--

*$p < .05$ **$p < .01$

Note. (7) = Hostility; (8) = Activity participation; (10) = Addresses personality; (11) = Accepts feelings; (12) = Encourages perspective-taking; (13) = Encourages independence

Table 7

Intracorrelations of TPOS Activity Codes

	Small group/ One child	Large group	Without Children	W/out ch. On-task	W/out ch. Off-task
(1) Small group/ One child	--	-.62**	-.04	-.11	-.36
(2) Large group		--	-.51	-.21	-.15
(3) Without children			--	.41	-.66**
(4) Without children/ On-task				--	.57**
(5) Without children/ Off-task					--

*p < .05 **p < .01

Table 8

Intracorrelations of TPOS Emotional Climate Classroom Codes

	(1) Emot. Climate	(2) T.is warm/respon	(3) T is inter/invol	(4) T is patient	(5) T. dis. pos. aff.	(6) T.div. time =
Emotional climate of the class-room	--	.46	.53*	.53**	.23	.23
Teacher is warm and responsive		--	.59**	.69**	.81**	.26
Teacher is interested and involved with the children			--	.94**	.62**	.44
Teacher is patient				--	.65**	.36
Teacher displays positive affect					--	.40
Teacher divides time equally among all children						--

*p < .05 **p < .01

Table 9

TPOS Intercorrelations of Group Size/Teacher Activity Codes with Teacher Behaviour Codes

	(1) Small Group	(2) Large Group	(3) Without Children	(4) W/out ch. On-task	(5) W/out ch. Off-task
(6) praise	.31	.30	-.66**	-.46	-.29
(7) hostility	.29	-.04	.10	.16	-.41
(8) activity participation	-.02	.34	-.51*	-.90**	-.30
(9) addresses behaviour	-.05	.43	-.11	-.18	-.62**
(10) addresses personality	-.20*	.65**	-.40	-.53*	-.55*
(11) accepts feelings	.18	.20	-.27	.09	-.18
(12) encourages perspective	-.00	.43	-.19	-.03	-.33
(13) encourages independence	.11	.14	-.15	-.25	-.18

*p < .05 **p < .01

Note. (4) = Without children/on-task; (5) = Without children/off-task

Table 10

TPOS Associations Between TPOS Teacher Behaviour Codes and Emotional Climate of Classroom

	(1) Emotional. Climate	(2) Teacher is warm & responsive	(3) Teacher interested & involved	(4) Teacher is patient	(5) Teacher displays positive affect	(6) Teacher divides time Equally
(6) praise	.16	.35	.51*	.45	.46	.10
(7) hostility	-.09	-.47*	-.19	-.29	-.49*	-.32
(8) activity participation	.33	.34	.50*	.44	.27	.01
(9) addresses behaviour	-.12	-.40	-.19	-.43	-.45	-.06
(10) addresses personality	.22	.00	.16	-.06	-.08	.02
(11) accepts feelings	.37	.22	.26	.12	.34	.53*
(12) encourages perspective	.01	.03	.10	-.06	-.01	.18
(13) encourages independence	.53*	.16	.28	.11	.08	.39

*p < .05 **p < .01

Table 11

Correlations Between TPOS Group-Size Codes/Teacher Activity and Emotional Climate of Classroom Codes

	Emot. Climate (1)	T. is warm & respon. (2)	T. is inter. & invol. (3)	T. is patient (4)	T. displays positive affect (5)	T. divides time equally (6)
(1) Small group	.03	.14	30	.32	.10	-.05
(2) Large group	.11	-.15	.14	-.04	-.05	.28
(3) Without Children	-.45	-.20	-.52*	-.46	-.16	-.33
(4) Without children on-task	-.48*	-.30	-.45	-.37	-.14	.12
(5) Without children Off-task	-.23	.17	-.22	-.03	.22	.06

*p < .05 **p <.01

Note. (1) = Emotional climate of the classroom (noise quality); (2) = Teacher is warm and responsive; (3) = Teacher is interested and involved with the children; (4) = Teacher is patient; (5) = Teacher displays positive affect; (6) = Teacher divides time equally among all children

Table 12

Correlations Between ECERS Activities Codes and TPOS Teacher Behavior Codes

	(6) PR	(7) HO	(8) AC.P.	(9) AD. BEH	(10) AD. PER	(11) ACC. FEEL	(12) ENC. P.TAK	(13) ENC. IND.
(3) Furniture for relaxation and comfort	.26	.26	.27	.14	.02	-.11	.01	-.11
(5) Space for privacy	-.19	.66**	-.45	.34	-.08	.28	.19	.25
(15) Books & Pictures	-.39	-.12	-.43	-.51*	-.75**	-.06	-.44	-.07
(19) Fine Motor	.51*	.01	-.02	-.40	-.33	.21	.06	-.06
(20) Art	-.21	.19	-.07	.12	-.00	-.20	.11	-.13
(21) Music/ movement	.39	.44	-.04	.19	-.09	.26	.28	.25
(22) Blocks	.14	.06	.01	-.19	-.14	-.07	-.07	-.10
(23) Sand/ water	.04	.06	-.20	-.31	-.30	-.08	-.08	-.02
(24) Dramatic play	.34	-.07	.21	-.26	-.12	-.07	-.07	-.06

(25) Nature/ science	-.08	-.81** .	.31	-.38	-.11	-.39	-.39	-.04
(26) Math/ number	-.33	-.28	-.22	-.16	-.21	-.35	-.35	.26
(28) Promoting acceptance of diversity								
Total Activities Scores	.20	.01	-.01	-.20	-.21	.19	-.04	.05

$*p < .05 **p < .01$

Note. (6) = Praise; (7) = Hostility; (8) = Activity participation; (9) = Addresses behaviour; (10) = Addresses personality; (11) = Accepts feelings; (12) = Encourages perspective-taking; (13) = Encourages independence

Table 13

Correlations Between ECERS Language Codes and TPOS Teacher Behaviour Codes

	(6) PR	(7) HOS	(8) AC. P.	(9) AD. BEH.	(10) ACC. PERS. TAK.	(11) ACC. FEEL.	(12) ENC. PERS. TAK.	(13) ENC. IND.
(9) Greeting/departing	--	--	--	--	--	--	--	--
(16) Encouraging to communicate	.62**	-.14	.38	-.00	.31	.50*	.35	.44
(17) Using language to develop reasoning skills	.19	-.36	.07	-.15	.12	.54*	.13	.23
(18) Informal use of language	.32	-.38	.24	-.06	.24	.57*	.25	.45
(30) General supervision of children	.48*	.25	.10	.26	.44	.57*	.65**	.29
(31) Discipline	.16	.16	.09	.26	.21	.25	.21	.01
(32) Staff-child interaction	--	--	--	--	--	--	--	--
(33) Interaction among children	--	--	--	--	--	--	--	--
(36) Group-time	--	--	--	--	--	--	--	--

$*p < .05 **p < .01$

Note. (6) = Praise; (7) = Hostility; (8) = Activity participation; (9) = Addresses behaviour; (10) = Addresses personality; (11) = Accepts feelings; (12) = Encourages perspective-taking; (13) = Encourages independence

Table 14

Intercorrelations Between ECERS Activity Codes and TPOS Group-Size/Teacher Activity Codes

	Small group (1)	Large group (2)	Without children (3)	Without ch./ontask (4)	Without Ch./offtask (5)
(3) Furniture for relaxation and comfort	.14	.17	-.35	-.23	-.17
(5) Space for privacy	.28	-.14	.09	.27	-.32
(19) Fine motor	.17	.02	-.32	.21	.22
(20) Art	-.29	.36	-.17	.16	-.01
(21) Music/movement	.35	-.09	.19	-.03	-.13
(22) Blocks	-.14	.36	-.33	.13	.22
(23) Sand/water	-.09	.19	-.07	.34	.36
(24) Dramatic play	-.01	.30	-.57*	-.05	.18

(25) Nature/science	-.31	.08	-.29	-.03	.54*
(26) Math/number	-.21	.01	.13	.34	.44
(28) Promoting acceptance Of diversity	.20	.07	.05	.25	.14
Total Activity Score	-.02	.24	-.32	.22	.32

$*p < .05 **p < .01$

Table 15

Correlations Between ECERS Language Scores and TPOS Group-Size/Teacher Activity Codes

	Small Group (1)	Large Group (2)	Without Children (3)	W/out Children On-task (4)	W/out Children Off-task (5)
(9) Greeting & departing	--	--	--	--	--
(15 Books & pictures	.02	-.32	.22	.59**	.55*
(16) Encouraging children To communicate	.28	.12	-.39	-.34	-.08
(17) Using language to develop reasoning skills	-.12	.24	-.23	.03	.24
(18) Informal use of language	.12	.17	-.40	-.13	-.03
(30) General supervision of children	.36	.16	-.28	-.20	-.38
(31) Discipline	.54*	-.28	.22	-.29	-.43
(32) Staff-child interaction	--	--	--	--	--

(33) Interactions among children	--	--	--	--	--
(36) Group-time	.41	-.14	-.09	-.35	-.23
Total Language Scores	.30	.02	-.26	-.05	.07

*p < .05 **p < .01

Table 16

Intercorrelations Between ECERS Activities Codes and TPOS Emotional Climate of the Classroom Codes

	Emot. Climate (1)	T. is warm & resp. (2)	T. is int. & involv. (3)	T. is pat. (4)	T. dis. pos. affect (5)	T. div. time equally between children (6)
(3) Furniture for relaxation and comfort	-.04	-.01	.16	.12	-.07	-.12
(5) Space for privacy	-.04	-.41	-.09	-.24	-.24	.10
(19) Fine motor	.06	.22	.21	.28	.36	.11
(20) Art	-.18	-.29	-.12	-.15	-.33	.10
(21) Music/movement	-.11	.09	.08	.00	.20	-.12
(22) Blocks	.12	.05	.29	.30	.09	.02
(23) Sand/water	.09	.11	.20	.25	.13	.02
(24) Dramatic play	.28	.27	.47*	.49*	.28	.09
(25) Nature/science	.13	.42	.25	.32	.37	.30
(26) Math/number	.17	.15	.08	.05	.16	.23

(28) Promoting acceptance of diversity	-.22	.05	.25	.19	.35	.21
Total Activities Score	.05	.16	.34	.31	.27	.21

*p < .05 **p < .01

Note. (1) = Emotional climate of the classroom (noise quality); (2) = Teacher is warm and responsive; (3) = Teacher is interested and involved with the children; (4) = Teacher is patient; (5) = Teacher displays positive affect; (6) = Teacher divides time equally among all children

Table 17

Intercorrelations Between ECERS Language Codes and TPOS Emotional Climate of the Classroom Codes

	Emot. climate (1)	T. is warm & resp. (2)	T. is int. & invol. (3)	T. is patient (4)	T. Displ. posit. affect (5)	T. divides time equally (6)
(9) Greeting/ Departing	---	--	--	--	--	--
(15) Books and pictures	-.10	.05	-.07	.05	.06	.12
(16) Encouraging children to communicate	.42	.74**	.62**	.55*	.65**	.30
(17) Using language to develop reasoning skills	.11	.30	.41	.29	.65**	.50*
(18) Informal use of language	.27	.33	.48*	.36	.52*	.69**
(30) General supervision of children	.13	.26	.54*	.37	.42	.31

(31) Discipline	-.09	.26	.54*	.09	.19	-.17
(32) Staff-child interaction	--	--	--	--	--	--
(33) Interaction among children	--	--	--	--	--	--
(36) Group-time	.29	.52*	.29	.25	.41	.10
Total Language Scores	.27	.61**	.61**	.51*	.75**	.54*

*$p < .05$ **$p < .01$

Note. (1) = Emotional climate of the classroom (noise quality); (2) = Teacher is warm and responsive; (3) = Teacher is interested and involved with the children; (4) = Teacher is patient; (5) = Teacher displays positive affect; (6) = Teacher divides time equally among all children

Table 18

Teacher Education Levels and Employment

Questions	Frequency	Percentage
1) Length of time working In the field		
a.) Less than a year	0	0%
b.) One-three years	2	11.1%
c.) Four-six years	6	33.3%
d.) Seven-ten years	4	22.2%
e.) More than ten years	6	33.3%
2.) Level of Education		
a.) High school leaving certificate	1	5.5%
b.) Some CEGEP courses	1	5.5%
c.) Attestation	8	44.4%
d.) Completion of DEC	5	27.7%
e.) Some university courses	1	5.5%
f.) Completion of undergraduate program	1	5.5%
g.) Graduate program	1	5.5%
3.) Reason for choosing to work in the ECE field		
a.) Love of children		50.0%

b.) Previous work experience	9	11.1%
c.) Preparation of parenthood	2	16.6%
d.) Convenience	3	5.5%
e.) Other	1	11.1%
f.) No answer	2	5.5%
	1	
4.) Length of time working at the centre		
a.) 0-24 months	3	16.0%
b.) 2-4 years	4	22.2%
c.) 5-6 years	4	33.3%
d.) 7-9 years	3	16.0%
e.) 10+ years	3	16.0%

Table 19

Classroom Play Structure Organization

Questions	Frequency	Percentage
5.) Number of Children in group		
a.) 7-8	12	66.6%
b.) 9-10	2	11.1%
c.) 14	2	11.1%
d.) 16	2	11.1%
6.) Center philosophy		
a.) Learning through play	9	50.0%
b.) High Scope/Reggio	3	16.6%
c.) Fairness, respect, autonomy	5	27.7%
d.) Take children's interests into consideration	1	5.5%
e.) Uncertain about philosophy	0	0%
f.) Other	2	11.1%
7.) Personal Philosophy		
a.) Learning through play, guiding	10	55.5%
b.) Instructivist (teacher-centred)	1	5.5%
c.) Children's interests and level of development taken	2	11.1%

into consideration		
d.) Children's enjoyment of program	2	11.1%
e.) Observing children	0	0%
f.) Other	2	11.1%
g.) No answer	1	5.5%

Table 20

Free Play and Structured Time

Questions	Frequency	Percentage
9.) Number of free play periods		
0	1	5.5%
1	12	66.6%
2	0	0%
3>	5	27.7%
10.) Length of free play periods		
0-15 minutes	1	5.5%
16-25 minutes	0	0
26-45 minutes	9	50%
46-60 minutes	4	22.2%
60> minutes	4	22.2%
21.) Number of structured play periods		
0	2	11.1%
1	9	50%
2	3	16.6%
3>	3	16.6%
No answer	1	5.5%

22.) Length of structured play periods		
0-15 minutes	3	16.6%
16-25 minutes	5	27.7%
26-45 minutes	5	27.7%
46-60 minutes	4	22.2%
60> minutes	1	5.5%
16.) Is free play an important part of your program?		
Yes	18	100%
No	0	0%
17.) What is your role during free play?		
a.) supporting play (guiding, facilitating)	12	66.6%
b.) teacher modeling appropriate behaviour	0	0%
c.) child autonomy (make decisions)	1	5.5%
d.) conflict resolution, problem-solving	7	38%
e.) redirecting inappropriate behaviour	1	5.5%
f.) other teacher responsibilities	3	16.6%
g.) other	7	38%
18.) During free play it is important for teachers to interact with children.		
strongly agree/agree	14	77.7%
neutral	1	5.5%
strongly disagree/disagree	2	11.1%

no response	1	5.5%
19.) During free play it is important for educators to observe children's play from a distance Strongly agree/agree Neutral Strongly disagree/disagree No response	 14 2 2	 77.7% 11.1% 11.1%
20.) Free play is as important as structured time Strongly agree/agree Neutral Strongly disagree/disagree	 18 0 0	 100% 0% 0%
23.) Describe what you do during a structured activity? a.) demonstrate b.) provide materials c.) give direction d.) follow children's lead e.) other What kind of structured activities do you do in you class? a.) Arts & crafts b.) Science c.) Cooking d.) Circle time (reading stories)	 9 12 7 1 1 7 5 3 4	 50.0% 66.6% 38.8% 5.5% 5.5% 38.8% 27.7% 16.6% 22.2%

e.) Table toys	0	0%
f.) Theme-related activities	0	0%
g.) Games	5	27.7%
h.) Other	4	22.2%
24.) Is it important to interact with children during structured play periods?		
Yes	14	77.7%
No	1	5.5%
Sometimes/maybe	1	5.5%
No response	2	11.1%
25.) Do you preselect materials for children during a structured activity?		
Yes	13	72.2%
No	0	0%
Sometimes/maybe	5	27.7%
28.) Structuring children's play is the best way to facilitate their learning and prepare them for school		
Strongly agree/agree		
	5	27.7%
Neutral		
	1	5.5%
Strongly disagree/disagree		
	12	66.6%
29.) Structuring children's play can limit their creativity and hinder their ability to make choices for themselves.		

Strongly agree/agree	14	77%
Neutral	0	0%
Strongly disagree/disagree	4	22%

Table 21

Teacher Beliefs and Attitudes

Question	Frequency	Percentage
11.) Are children able to play with any material they want?		
Yes	17	94.4%
No	0	0
Sometimes	1	5.5%
12.) Is it alright for children to combine materials?		
Yes	18	100%
No	0	0%
13.) Are children able to play with the same material for more than 1 free play period?		
Yes	18	100%
No	0	0%
14.) Do you believe that teachers should limit the length of time children can play with certain toys or materials?		
Yes	2	11.1%
No	15	83.3%
Sometimes/maybe	1	5.5%
15.) Do you believe that teachers should limit the length of time children can play in one particular area or participate in an activity?		

Yes	10	55.5%
No	6	33.3%
Sometimes/maybe	2	11.1%
26.) Do children need to be told what to do in order to learn?		
Yes	2	11.1%
No	12	66.6%
Sometimes	4	22.2%
27.) When structuring children's play is it important that all children participate?		
Yes	2	11.1%
No	16	88.8%
27a.) If children don't want to?		
a.) Strongly encourage children	7	38.8%
b.) Repeat activity	2	11.1%
c.) Let them engage in another activity	11	61.1%
31.) Should children be left alone to play in the way they choose without adult involvement or should teachers engage themselves in children's play?		
a.) leave children alone		
b.) adult involvement		
32.) What does it mean to guide children's play?		
a.) offer choices	3	16.6%
b.) assist in language development and conflict resolution	4	22.2%

c.) support children's interaction with others	3	16.6%
d.) provide developmentally appropriate materials and toys	1	5.5%
e.) facilitate, scaffold play	8	44.4%
f.) observe	1	5.5%
g.) develop positive relationships with children and establish goals	0	0%
h.) support growth and development	3	16.6%
33.) Is it important to guide children's play to help them learn?		
Yes	10	55.5%
No	5	27.7%
Sometimes	3	16.6%
34.) Is there a difference between structuring and guiding children's play?		
Yes	16	88.8%
No	1	5.5%
Sometimes	1	5.5%
35.) What is the best aspect of your program?		
a.) diversity	1	5.5%
b.) outdoor facilities	1	5.5%
c.) personal characteristics of educator, positive environment	4	22.2%
d.) ambience of the centre, family-oriented (good staff relationships)	2	11.1%
e.) child-centred program	8	44.4%

f.) other	2	11.1%
36.) What is the most important part of an early childhood educator's job?		
a.) Foster positive relationships with children	5	27.7%
b.) Maintain safe, secure environment	3	16.6%
c.) Awareness of children's strengths and abilities	0	0%
d.) Love of field and children	6	33.3%
e.) Guide and educate children	6	33.3%
f.) Other	3	16.6%
37.) Can you talk about one part of your day that occurred, while I was here, that was especially significant?		
a.) Teacher-centred	7	38.8%
b.) Child-centred	8	44.4%
c.) Other	2	11.1%
d.) No response	1	5.5%

Table 22

Correlations between Interview Questionnaire Responses and ECERS Language and Activity Codes

Interview Question	Interview Response	Total ECERS Activity & Language Scores
16.) Is free play an important part of your program?	c.) home-away-from-home	-.49[t]
17.) What is your role during free play?	a.) supporting play (guiding, faciliatating)	.57*
17.) What is your role during free play?	c.) child autonomy (making decisions)	-.69**
32.) What does it mean to guide children's play?	e.) facilitate, scaffold play, extend play	.59**
37.) Can you talk about one part of your day that occurred while I was here that was especially significant?	b.) Child-centred	.40

[t] $p < .10$* $p < .05$ ** $p < .01$

Table 23

Correlations between Interview Questionnaire Responses and ECERS Language Codes

Interview Question	Interview Response	ECERS Language Score
16.) Is free play an important part of your program?	c.) home-away-from-home	$-.49^t$
16.) Is free play an important part of your program?	d.) teacher observation of children	$-.40^t$
17.) What is your role during free play?	c.) child autonomy, making decisions	$-.51^*$
32.) What does it mean to guide children's play?	e.) facilitate, scaffold play, extend play	$.59^{**}$

$^t p < .10$ $^* p < .05$ $^{**} p < .01$

Table 24

Correlations between Interview Questionnaire Responses and ECERS Activity Codes

Interview Question	Interview Response	ECERS Activity Score
16.) Is free play an important part of your program?	d.) teacher observation of children	-.57*
17.) What is your role during free play?	c.) child autonomy, making decisions	-.56*

* $p < .05$

Discussion

The purpose of this section is to discuss the key findings, which were presented in the results section and that are pertinent to the hypotheses put forth in the present study. Second, a picture of the teachers' background and classroom structure is provided. The findings related to the ECERS are discussed followed by the findings related to the TPOS scale and lastly the Interviews, which were conducted with the educators will be discussed. In sum, the most significant findings were the impact that teacher's language and communication styles had on the classroom atmosphere. This finding will be discussed at greater length in the following sections. Teachers who engaged in positive communication and encouraged children to talk and share their perspectives did have classrooms with warm positive atmospheres. Another key finding was that many educators reported having a strong value for free play. Many educators, however, felt under pressure from directors and parents for children to produce something to prove that they were learning something. This supports research put forth in the present study by Charlesworth et al. (1993), which stated that educators found it difficult to balance their beliefs with pressure from parents to create an academic structure in their classrooms.

Who were the Teachers?

The majority of teachers had been working in the field for over four years. There was only eleven percent who had been working in the field for between one and three years. The majority of teachers had completed an attestation or a DEC in early childhood education. Many wanted to work in the field because they were passionate about, and loved children. All the teachers felt strongly that free play was a valuable experience for children. The reasons for its importance included; helping children learn to make decisions, encouraging creativity, allowing children the opportunity to discover what they liked to do. Some felt that structured play was more effective to help prepare children for school and as such was more appropriate for preschool children than toddlers.

The teacher interview was designed to tap educator's views on free play and structured play. There were a variety of questions that probed the importance that teachers placed on the two types of play. One key issue was that the educators had a difficult time defining their own personal philosophies, although more than half supported a learning-through-play perspective! Many of the educators were able to define the philosophy of the centers but were vague in terms of their own philosophy. This supports research by Charlesworth et al. (1991), who stated that when educators were interviewed they expressed their beliefs in vague terms rather than supporting specific theoretical beliefs. Terms that are associated with constructivism were mentioned (e.g. scaffolding), but none of the educators stated that they subscribed to a constructivist philosophy although they were aware that there was a difference between guiding and structuring children's play. Many educators felt that structure implied rigidity, whereas guiding was defined more as following the child's lead. Educators stated that it was important to guide children to help them develop their play, however none of the educators used the term "scaffolding" in this sense.

All the teachers involved in the present study felt that free play was a valuable part of their program and was as important as structured activities. When questioned about the length of time children spent engaging in free play one educator stated that she had to limit free play time due to scheduling issues because of sharing of space with other groups. Other educators mentioned issues with directors wanting children to produce things to demonstrate their learning was also an issue. Half the educators had between

26-45 minutes of free play each day. Four reported between 46-60 minutes and an equal

number reported more than 60 minutes a day. Only one educator stated that she had only

15 minutes of free play a day. All the educators expressed a strong appreciation for the

value of free play time, however, they were often unable to allow children the freedom to

engage in the kind of free play they wanted children to have or for the length of time they

wanted for a variety of reasons. Time, space and parent/director expectations were

frequently cited reasons for the limited free play. This supports research (Moyer,

Egertson & Isenberrg; 1987; Charlesworth et al., 1991), which stated that often teachers

reported having to compromise their beliefs because of parental and managerial

expectations.

Quality of the Childcare Environment

  Intracorrelations of the ECERS Activities subscale. The purpose of this section is to

discuss the correlations found between the ECERS Activities and Language scores and,

how they relate to the hypotheses put forth in the present study. First, the

intercorrelations on the Activities subscale showed many of the items were positively

related. For example, significant correlations were found between sand/water, dramatic

play and blocks. These correlations demonstrate that the majority of the centers who

participated in the present study did have these four components in their programs. That

is, centers that received high rating on sand/water were also likely to receive high scores

for dramatic play and blocks. This indicates that centers that have some open-ended

materials tend to have a variety of open-ended play materials, providing children with

various opportunities for self-directed free play. This supports the argument put forth by the present study that high quality centers would tend to provide children with open-ended materials and reflect developmentally appropriate practice.

The ECERS Language subscale. The inability to correlate the scores for *Greeting/Departing, Staff/Child interaction* and *Interaction among the children* due to the fact that there was no variability and all the centres received high scores could also support the high quality of the centres involved with the present study. In terms of the ECERS Language subscale there were positive correlations found with encouraging children to communicate and general supervision of children and group-time. This supports the hypothesis that teachers who are involved and aware of what is going on in their classroom would tend to support and encourage children to communicate and develop their language skills.

Second the intracorrelations on the Language subscale indicated positive correlations between teachers, when they were supervising a group of children, were also likely to develop reasoning skills and to use language informally. This supports the hypothesis put forth by the present study. Specifically, it had been proposed that teachers who engaged in developmentally appropriate practices would engage in behaviour that would facilitate children's cognitive and language development by using language in an informal, casual manner and would interact and talk more with children, encouraging them to reason problems out for themselves instead of solving problems for them. This finding is supported by prior literature. For example, children often create problems in their play opportunities and with the guidance of their teachers are able to improve their language skills and their problem solving capabilities (Yang, 2000). Other research discussed in the present study further supported the importance of teacher involvement in children's play to help children learn to negotiate and become confident in their own problem solving capabilities (Klein et al., 2003).

   The ECERS Activities and Language subscales. Correlations were also examined between items on the Activities and the Language subscales. One interesting set of findings revealed positive correlations between discipline, group-time and music/movement. This could be viewed as another piece of evidence demonstrating that problematic behaviour is more likely to arise when children are required to engage in a structured group activity, which they have not chosen. A high score in the discipline category does not demonstrate negative teacher behavour, it does, however, show that more sitiuations arise that require the teacher to discipline the children in some manner. This would substantiate the argument that there are fewer behavioral problems when children are in environments that are child-centred and in which they are free to choose to participate in an activity.

   The correlations between group-time, encouraging children to communicate and discipline suggests that teachers use group-time to engage children in conversation and perhaps in resolving conflict. The fact that discipline is correlated with group-time supports the previous argument that there may be more behavioural problems when children are required to participate in an activity.

   Music/movement was correlated with teacher's encouraging children to communicate suggesting that teachers may involve children in singing songs, and other musical activities. Certainly, the correlation between group-time and music/movement suggests that many educators engage in musical activities with large groups of children. Music/movement and discipline were also correlated further supporting the idea that requiring or "strongly encouraging" children to participate in group activities may be

associated with discipline problems.

In conclusion one of the key findings was that disciplinary issues tended to be

associated with large group activities more than small group situations that were likely to

be observed during free play. This could be viewed as support for the argument put forth

that behavioural problems are more likely to occur when children are required to

participate in activities than when they are given free choice. The concept of allowing

children to choose freely to participate in activities was advocated by researchers who

raised the fact that teachers who engaged in developmentally appropriate practice would

provide children with a variety of activities from which they chould freely select (Klein et

al., 2003).

Total ECERS Activities and Language Scores. There was no correlation found

between the two subscales. This demonstrates that the items represented by the two

subscales function independently of one another. With regard to the Language subscale it

should be noted that English was not the first language of some of the teachers and this

factor could have impacted their ability to communicate and converse with children. This

will be discussed further in the future research section.

Quality of Teacher-Child Interaction

The next area of discussion is the correlations found between the TPOS teacher

behaviour measures, and how they relate to the present study.

First, the intracorrelations of the teacher behaviour variables were interesting. The

positive correlation between praise and activity participation indicates that teachers who

engage in activity with children seemed to use positive reinforcement. This supports the idea that teachers who told children what to do but did not engage in activities would have a less positive classroom atmosphere than those educators who engaged themselves with the children. It may be that the former teachers held an instructivist philosophy, whereas the later teachers subscribed to a more constructivist philosophy. This is a point which will be discussed in more detail at a later point in the discussion. It also supports the research of Kontos (1999) who discussed the importance of educators' supporting children's play to encourage longer and more intensive investigation. By being engaged teachers may be able to use praise as a way to support children's learning.

The strong positive correlation found between teachers who addressed behaviour and those who addressed personality issues (e.g., teacher telling children to be quiet, teacher telling children that they are lazy.), suggested that some teachers may notice and address many of the children's actions in their classroom. The correlation between teachers who address personality and those who encourage perspective-taking also suggests that teachers who encourage perspective-taking appear to address the individual character of the child that he/she is talking to in the classroom. This is logical since a teacher who is encouraging a child to verbalize something from their perspective may ask for their opinion. This style of communication is important as it demonstrates that the teacher is attempting to encourage the child's cognitive development, and may be using a scaffolding technique. This would support the hypothesis arguedu by the present study that teachers in high quality centres which rated well on the ECERS measure, would tend to support developmentally appropriate practices.

Intracorrelations of TPOS teacher behaviours. First, there were a substantial number of strong positive intracorrelations between teacher's affective behaviour demonstrating that there was a link between the teacher's positive behaviours; that is, if a teacher is positive in one aspect, he/she will most likely have other attributes that assist in creating a positive classroom environment (for example, smiling at children, getting down to the child's physical level, using a friendly tone of voice, offering praise and encouragement to children). This supports research by Moulton et al. (1999), which mentioned that educators who were positive in one behavioural aspect would tend to be positive in others as well. Educators are not likely to be smiling at children and yelling at them or engaging in play and speaking in a derogatory manner at the same time.

Second, the intracorrelations of the TPOS Activity codes were self-evident. Teachers who were interacting with a large group of children were not likely to be interacting with a small group. When teachers were being observed without children they were not observed being with children. Logically the negative correlations are self-explanatory as it would be physically impossible for teachers to be with and without children at the same time or with a large group and a small group at the same time. These findings do provide a measure of face validity for the TPOS measure.

Third, the correlations between teacher behaviour and activity codes revealed some interesting patterns. The negative correlation between teachers who were interacting with a small group of children and addressing personality issues was found and a significant positive correlation between teachers interacting with a large group of children and addressing personality issues. These correlations support the hypothesis that the quality of interactions decline when the teacher/children ratio is high versus when teachers are interacting with individual children or a small group of children. This correlation coupled with the correlations found between discipline and group-time and music discussed earlier, further supports the argument that behavioural problems are more likely to occur in large group-time activities, especially those in which children are required to participate.

Fourth, the associations between teacher behavior and emotional climate were examined. The negative correlations found between hostility and the warmth and responsiveness of the teacher and the demonstration of positive affect by the teacher supported the argument that teachers who were warm, involved, and positive were less likely to engage in sarcastic, demeaning, and hostile behaviour. The positive correlation between teachers' acceptance of children's feelings and dividing time equally amongst all the children could be evidence that teachers who are accepting of children's feelings do not play favourites with the children. The positive correlation between a positive emotional climate in the classroom and teachers who encouraged children to be independent supports the argument put forth by the present study that teachers who create a warm, positive environment will encourage children to try and do things for themselves and reinforce their efforts. Research indicates that children attending developmentally inappropriate, academic-type preschool programs with children who did not perform as well socially as children who attended children attending developmentally appropriate programs (Burt et al., 1992).

Associations between TPOS Activity codes and Emotional Climate. With regard to this area there were some self-explanatory correlations such as the negative correlation between praise and teacher's being without children. Other correlations are more interesting. A negative correlation was found between teachers who addressed children's personality and small group size and a positive correlation was found between teachers

who addressed children's personality issues and large group size. These correlations
support the argument that there would be more negative behaviour and more
admonishments from teachers when they were dealing with large groups of children as
opposed to smaller sized groups of children. These findings support prior work that
stated that educators of large groups of children were more likely to engage in
developmentally inappropriate practices than educators interacting with small groups of
children (Buchanan et al., 1998).

Quality of the Environment and Teacher Behaviour

The next area of discussion is the correlations found between the quality of the
environment as rated by the ECERS and the teacher behaviour ratings of the TPOS scale.
It was expected that classrooms that received high scores on the ECERS would be
positively associated with teachers who were rated as having positive characteristics on
the TPOS scale.

First, the positive correlation between hostility and classes that have a space for
privacy is disconcerting, demonstrating that possibly these spaces are used as places for
teachers to engage in hostile behaviour towards a child without being seen. There was
also a strong negative correlation between nature/science and hostility. This may suggest
that teachers who have a strong interest in nature and science are less likely to engage in
hostile behaviour than teachers who do not demonstrate an interest in natural sciences or
that teachers who reprimand a lot do not have many science materials in their classrooms.
There was also a negative correlation between books and pictures and teachers who
addressed behaviour and personality. This correlation suggests that there is little
interaction between teachers and children when they are looking at books, suggesting that

perhaps teachers use books as babysitters for children when they are occupied or engaged

in other activities. In sum, these correlations suggest that teachers engage in negative

behaviour, at a minimal level of interaction when children are looking at books or are

involved in nature/science activities. There is no literature available in this area to

determine if others have reported similar findings.

Secondly, there was also a correlation between fine motor activities and praise. It is

interesting to note that there is a correlation between fine motor activities and praise, but

not with any other area. This may suggest that teachers enjoy engaging in fine motor

activities and tend to positively reinforce children who participate in these activities.

Perhaps teachers spent more time sitting at art tables engaging in art activities than in

other areas of the classroom (e.g., sitting on the floor playing with blocks) and therefore

have more opportunities to praise. This may be a question that could be addressed in

future research.

Third, the positive correlation between general supervision and praise is logical in that

teachers would have to be aware of what is going on in their classroom to be able to

praise children. Encouraging children to communicate and praise were also positively

correlated. Encouraging children to communicate and developing autonomy are

behaviours, which teachers who employ developmentally appropriate practices try to

facilitate in their classroom (Moulton et al., 1999). They would be characteristic of a

child-centred classroom, thus supporting the hypothesis that teachers who have child-

centred classrooms would be more involved in children's play than instructivist teachers.

The cluster of positive correlations between teachers who accepted children's feelings,

encouraged children to communicate, used language to develop reasoning skills, and employed informal use of language and engaged in general supervision of children

supports the argument that constructivist teachers would engage in behaviour that would

create a positive atmosphere in which children would be encouraged to be empathetic and

their perspective would be considered. This supports research (Howes & Smith, 1995),

which stated that good teachers would engage in a high level of positive verbal

interaction and a minimal amount of criticism and few negative comments. The

researchers went on to stress that teachers who engage in positive verbal and social

interaction with children have classes in which children feel securely attached to their

teachers. Howes and Smith (1995) demonstrated that children who were emotionally

secure with their teachers engaged in high levels of positive social interaction.

    Associations between TPOS Activity and ECERS Activity codes. First, a positive

correlation was found between children engaging in dramatic play and teachers who were

patient, involved and interested which supports the argument stated by the present study.

This finding is also in line with Zeece and Graul (1990) and Rothstein and Brett, (1987)

that teacher involvement does develop and enhance the play of children. The negative

correlation between dramatic play and the teacher leaving the room (being without

children) further supports the impact that teacher presence has on children's play,

specifically even if teachers are not involved in play, their presence or absence has an

impact on it. This supports research (Smilansky & Shefatya, 1990) which demonstrated a

significant increase in the level of children's play when adults became involved in

children's play. This could be due to the fact that children who have a secure emotional

attachment to their teacher enjoy interaction and involvement with their teacher. Other

research (Mellou, 1994) suggested that children mirror their teacher's behaviour. The fact that the children lost interest in the play when the teacher left the room offers support for the belief that teacher presence has a strong impact on the development of children's play.

Associations between ECERS Activity codes and TPOS Activity codes. First, correlations were evident between nature/science and teachers being without children and off-task, which could demonstrate that children tend to engage in this type of behaviour when the teacher is not present and interacting with the children. No significant correlations were found between the Total ECERS Activity scores and the TPOS teacher Activity codes. This could be due to the small sample size.

Associations between ECERS Language Codes and TPOS Teacher Activity codes. First, correlations were found between teachers being without children but on-task, being without children and off-task and books and pictures. This pattern of findings could demonstrate that teachers use books to occupy children when they must engage in classroom related activities or when they are chatting with coworkers or if they have to leave the room for brief periods of time. It could be that books are also used as an activity to occupy children during transition times. A significant positive correlation was found between small group size and discipline. It would have been interesting to note if it was the same children who the teacher addressed concerning personality issues during large group time. This could be an area of further study.

Associations between ECERS Activity Items and TPOS Emotional Climate of the Classroom. In relation to the Activities component, dramatic play was the only activity which demonstrated a significant correlation with teachers being interested and involved with the children's play and with teachers who exhibited patience with children. This could be due to the fact that while the centers did have the facilities for children to engage in other forms of play such as with sand and water, that dramatic play was the most frequent open-ended play that was available for children during the researcher's visits. The correlation between teachers who exhibited patience and who were interested and involved with children's play supports the argument that teachers with positive attributes would be more likely to engage themselves in the children's play than teachers with more negative characteristics.

ECERS Language Scores and TPOS Emotional Climate. In relation to the language codes and the emotional climate there were a substantial number of correlations. Encouraging children to communicate was positively correlated with teachers who were warm, responsive, patient, involved with children and who showed positive affect towards the children. This pattern of correlations supports the belief that teachers who demonstrated a positive, enthusiastic disposition will engage in behaviours that help scaffold children's learning (i.e., speaking to children in a way that helps them develop their language skills.). The correlation between teachers who divided their time equally amongst all the children and the informal use of language suggested that teachers who circulate between all the children in their class during free play tend to chat with them in a casual manner. Using language to develop reasoning skills was also significantly correlated with teachers' demonstration of positive affect supporting the argument that teachers who engage in constructivist practices, such as scaffolding children's cognitive development would be more positive than teachers who engaged in more instructivist practices.

The positive correlation between teachers who accept children's feelings, encourage perspective-taking and the level of general supervision indicates that if teachers are observing and aware of what is going on in their classrooms they are more likely to listen to what children have to say and encourage them to try and see situations from different perspectives.

Finally, discipline was correlated with teachers who were interested and involved with children, suggesting that teachers, even those with constructivist-style classrooms, still use discipline as the most common means of keeping control of children's behaviour. High scores in the discipline component of the ECERS does not mean that teachers are engaging in negative behaviour, rather discipline is considered to involve the children in conflict resolution and problem solving. Thus, high scores support the belief that teachers who believed in constructivist principles would tend to engage in positive classroom behaviour, such as scaffolding children's conflict resolution skills.

In conclusion, the high number of positive correlations between language and the emotional climate of the classroom supports the idea put forth by the present study that teachers who talk in a warm, positive manner, and encourage children to express their opinions will have classrooms with more positive atmospheres than teachers with instructivist, teacher-directed classes.

Associations between Child Care Quality and Teacher Beliefs

In relation to the associations between child care quality and teacher beliefs, the hypothesis put forth by the present study that educators who subscribed to a constructivist philosophy would engage in more developmentally appropriate practices was not supported entirely. Many educators believed in developmentally appropriate practices but their implementation was not as strong as their beliefs. This supports research (Maxell, 2001), which stated that there was a significant discrepancy between educator beliefs and practices. This could be because directors of some child care centres may not have a background in early childhood education and as such may not be aware of what is developmentally appropriate for children or perhaps they view their centres as businesses and focus on keeping the parents, who also may not be aware of what is appropriate for children, happy.

Limitations of the Present Study

One of the key limitations of the present study was its small sample size, which does limit the level of internal reliability and generalisability of findings. Another limitation was that on some of the observation visits some children were absent from the class, which could have had an impact on the classroom dynamics and on the teacher's behaviors. The third limitation was that the interview used in the present study was a self-report tool, so the educators could report what they knew were the appropriate responses to the questions in an effort to ensure a high social desirability factor. This fact, coupled with the limited observations (two-30 minute observations) meant that educators could try and create the façade of a developmentally appropriate classroom. The researcher was sensitive to this issue and evidence of this was found in only one of the classrooms during one of the observation periods where the teacher offered the children the opportunity to select the story that they wanted her to read. One child replied "but you never let us choose the book!" The educator replied that they were trying something new on this particular occasion. It should be stressed that this was the only instance of this type of behaviour and all the other educators did seem to maintain or demonstrate a genuine and natural disposition, which was not contrived.

The final limitation of the present study, which needs to be addressed, is the selection of centres for the purpose of this study. All the centers that participated were affiliated with a local college's early childhood education program. This means that the centers tended to reflect a higher quality of center than may be typical in Montreal. Unfortunately daycare centers that are more atypical, and might be of a lower quality of care, were contacted but declined to participate in the study.

Implications for Practice. Three major points stand out from the analyses that have implications for practice.

Language skills of educators. After analyzing the correlations and determining the significant correlations between language and the emotional climate of classrooms, it becomes obvious that strong language skills are a necessity for creating positive early childhood learning environments. Given this fact, directors should ensure that the teachers they employ have the capability to converse freely and effectively with children. Colleges and universities, which accredit early childhood education students, should also ensure that students have adequate language skills to converse and lead discussions with children, prior to the completion of their programs.

Training of directors. After reviewing the interview questionnaire responses it was noted that the training of centre managers is an issue that needs to be assessed. Currently two-thirds of educators must be qualified in a child care centre. There is no specific educational or training requirement for directors. This is an issue which needs to be addressed since it is the directors of the centres who set the standards for educators to

follow.

Classroom space. An issue that was mentioned by some educators was the lack of

space for children to leave projects for a few days and scheduling problems whereby

children had limited time for free play because of sharing the class with other groups of

children. When planning programs and schedules it would be important for teachers to

discuss classroom arrangements that would allow children the time and space necessary

to develop and extend their play.

Future Research

The topic of free play is not a particularly well-researched area, and in general

deserves to be studied at greater length. Of particular interest would be to look at the

impact private space has on the teacher's behaviour. Since having private space for

children is seen as a positive characteristic of a classroom (e.g., ECERS), it warrants

further investigation to determine if that space is being utilized in a positive manner.

The TPOS was an excellent and well-thought out observational tool that could be used

in future research, and it worked well in collaboration with the ECERS. In future

research it is recommended that teachers be observed for more than two 30-minute

periods, and that observations of both free play and structured activity periods be

included. This would help give a better overview of the program structure and teacher-

child interactions.

Future studies could also look at the impact that daycare director's beliefs have on

classroom practices. It would be interesting to look at whether daycare directors with

academic or business backgrounds encourage educators to engage in different classroom practices than directors with early childhood education training. Directors with early

childhood education training may be more likely to encourage educators to engage in

developmentally appropriate practices, whereas those with training in other domains may

be more likely to be more concerned with appearances and having children "produce"

something to impress parents with.

Another area of future research that could be interesting to examine would be to look

at educator's behavior when engaging in play with children. It would be interesting to

research whether educators are encouraging child-centered or teacher-centred play when

they are involved in children's activity; a more fine-grained analysis of teacher behaviour

during free play periods, small group and large group activities is warranted.

A final area of future study could also research the connection between praise and fine

motor activities versus praise and gross motor activities and examine the relationship

from a gender perspective. For example, the results showed a link between praise and

fine motor activity but none between praise and gross motor activity. Future research

could examine the amount of time boys and girls spend engaging in gross motor and fine

motor activity and, then analyze the amount of time teachers spent engaging with the

children in the two forms of activity and whether there was a discrepancy between the

amount of praise boys and girls received.

Conclusion

In conclusion, these analyses demonstrate that teachers who are involved and

communicate effectively with children do encourage language development and

reasoning skills. It also shows that teachers can support children's language development

by communicating with them in an informal manner, typical of a constructivist teacher, instead of in a structured formal type of speech, which may be more typically found in an instructivist setting. The analyses also support the argument that discipline issues are more likely to arise when children are required to participate in an activity, and especially when large groups of children are brought together to engage in a teacher-chosen activity. The main conclusion which can be drawn from this research is that the teacher's interactions with children do have an impact on children's play. The language and attitudes of the teachers also are critical in the atmosphere of the classroom atmosphere. There also appear to be more behavioural issues when large groups of children are engaged in an activity. This is a point which should be kept in mind when teachers are structuring activities for their class programs. It also could demonstrate the importance of having teachers consider the individual interests and needs of the children and incorporate them into their programs. Another point is that teachers should be aware of what is going on their classrooms and should ensure that they participate in all activities equally, not focusing their attention only on arts and other fine motor activities. The final point, which is important, is that while the ECERS states what the necessary components are for a classroom to have a good rating it does not discuss the importance of how those components are incorporated. For example, with regards to the space for privacy it would be important to ensure that space is being utilized for positive purposes. While the ECERS is an excellent tool for measuring the quality of the classroom, another tool must be used to measure the teacher behaviour to gain a more complete overview of the quality of the classroom environment as a whole.

References

Barclay, K., & Bernelli, C. (1995/96). Program evaluation through the eyes of a child. *Childhood Education*, Winter, 91-96.

Berk, L. (1985). Relationship of caregiver education to child-oriented attitudes, job satisfaction, and behaviors toward children. *Child Care Quarterly*, Summer, 103-129.

Burts, D., Hart, H., Charlesworth, R., Fleege, P., Mosley, J., & Thomasson, R. (1992). Observed activities and stress behaviors of children in developmentally appropriate and inappropriate kindergarten classrooms. *Early Childhood Research Quarterly, 7*, 297-318.

Bruce, T. (1993). The role of play in children's lives. *Childhood Education*, 237-238.

Buchanan, T., Burts, D., Bidner, J., White F., & Charlesworth, R. (1988). Predictors of the developmental appropriateness of the beliefs and practices of first, second and third grade teachers, *Early Childhood Research Quarterly, 13*, 459-483.

Cassidy, D., Buell, M., Pugh-Hoese, S., & Russell, S. (1995). The effect of education on child care teachers' beliefs and classroom quality: Year one evaluation of the TEACH early childhood associate degree scholarship program. *Early Childhood Research Quarterly, 10*, 171-183.

Chaille, C., & Silvern, S.B. (1996). Understanding through play. *Childhood Education, 72*, 274-277.

Charlesworth, R., Hart, C., Burts, D. (1991). Kindergarten teachers beliefs and practices. *Early Child Development and Care, 70* 17-35.

Charlesworth, R., Hart, C., Burts, D., Thomasson, R., Mosley, J., Fleege, P. (1993).

Measuring the developmental appropriateness of kindergarten teachers' beliefs and

practices. *Early Childhood Research Quarterly, 8,* 255-276.

Christie, J., Johnsen, E., & Peckover, R. (1988). The effects of play period duration on

children's play patterns patterns. *Journal of Research in Childhood Education, 3,*

123- 131.

Davey Zeece, P., & Graul, S. (1990). Learning to play: playing to learn. *Day Care and*

Early Education, Autumn, 11-15.

Feitelson, D., & Ross, G.S. (1973). The neglected factor-play, *Human Development,*

16, 202-223.

File, N., & Gullo, D. (2002). A comparison of early childhood and elementary

education students' beliefs about primary classroom teaching practices. *Early*

Childhood Research Quarterly, 17, 126-137.

Hatch, J., & Freeman, E. (1988). Kindergarten philosophies and practices: perspectives

of teachers, principals, and supervisors. *Early Childhood Research Quarterly, 3,*

151-166.

Howes, C., & Smith, E. (1995). Relations among child care quality, teacher

behavior, children's play activities, emotional security, and cognitive activity in

child care. *Early Childhood Research Quarterly, 10,* 381-404.

Isenberg, J. (1990). Teacher's thinking and beliefs and classroom practice. *Childhood*

Education, 322-327.

Jambor, T. (1996). *Dimensions of play: Reflections and directions,* IPA World

Conference.

Johnson, J.E. et al, (1999). *Play and early child development.* Chapter 9: Play

 Environments.

Kagan, D., & Smith, K. (1988). Beliefs and behaviours of kindergarten teachers.

 Educational Research, 30(1), 26-35

Kagan, D. (1992). Implications of research on teacher belief. *Educational*

 Psychologist, 27, 65-90.

Klein, T., Wirth, D., & Linas, K. (2003). Play children's context for development,

 Spotlight on Young Children and Play, May, 2003, 28-34.

Kontos, S., & Kayes, L. (1999), An ecobehavioral analysis of early childhood

 classrooms, *Early Childhood Research Quarterly, 14*, 35-50.

Leeseman, P., Rollenberg, L., & Rispens, J. (2001). Playing and working in

 kindergarten: Cognitive co-construction in two educational situations. *Early*

 Childhood Research Quarterly, 16, 363-384.

Marcon, R.A. (1999). Differential impact of preschool models on developmental and

 early learning of inner-city children: a three cohort study. *Developmental Psychology,*

 35, 358-375.

Maxwell, K., McWilliam, R.A., Hemmetter, M.L., Jones Ault, M., & Schuster, J.W.

 (2001). Predictors of developmentally appropriate classroom practices in

 kindergarten through third grade. *Early Childhood Research Quarterly, 16*, 431-

 452.

Mellou, E.. (1994). Tutored-untutored dramatic play: similarities and differences,

 Early Child Development and Care, 100, 119-130.

Moulton, C., Coplan, R., & Mills, C. (1999). The teaching practices observation scale (TPOS): an observational taxonomy for assessing teacher-preschool interactions during free play. *Canadian Journal of Research in Early Childhood Education, 8,* 19-29.

Moyer, J., Egertson, H., & Isenberg, J. (1987). The child-centered kindergarten, *Childhood Education, April,* 235-242.

Palincsar, A.S. (1998). Social constructivist perspectives on teaching and learning. *Annual Review Psychology, 49,* 345-375.

Reifel, S., & Yeatman, J. (1993). From category to context: reconsidering classroom play, *Early Childhood Research Quarterly, 8,* 347-367.

Ruben, K., Fein, G., & Vandenberg, B. (1983). Handbook of child psychology, NY: Wiley, P. Mussen (Ed.)

Stollar, S., & Dye Collins, P. (1994). Structured free-play to reduce disruptive activity changes in a head start classroom. *School Psychology Review, 23,* 310-324.

Summers, M., Stroud, J.C., Stroud, J.E., & Heaston, A. (1991). Preschoolers' perceptions of teacher role and importance. *Early Child Development and Care, 68,* 125-131.

Tegano, D., Sawyers, J., & Moran, J. (1989). Problem-finding and solving in play: The teacher's Role. *Childhood Education, Winter,* 92-97.

Vartulli, S. (1999). How early childhood teachers beliefs vary across grade level *Early Childhood Research Quarterly, 14,* 489-514.

Vartulli, S. (2005). Beliefs: the heart of teaching. *Young Children, September,* 76-86

Yang, S.O. (2000). Guiding children's verbal plan and evaluation during free play: An application of Vgotsky's genetic epistemology to the early childhood classroom. *Early Childhood Education Journal, 28,* 3-10.

http:www.statcan.ca/Daily/English/050207/d050207b.htm

Appendix A

Definitions and Examples of Teacher Interactions on the TPOS

Category	Example
(1) Small Group/Individual Interaction	Teacher is interacting with between one and five children.
(2) Large group interactions	Teacher is interacting with five or more children.
(3) Ontask	Teacher is (1) setting up an activity, but not interacting with the children; (2) observing the children from a distance, and (3) moving around the class, interacting with the children and observing their play and activities.
(4) Offtask	Any time when the teacher is engaged in behaviour that is totally unrelated to the children, such as chatting with other adults, talking on the phone, or writing at the counter.
(a) Praise and encouragement	(e.g., "you're trying really hard to put that shoe on. It looks like it's almost on your foot.")
(b) Activity participation	(e.g., teacher is engaging in activity with children; playing with playdough, helping build block tower, etc.)
(c) Hostility	(e.g., using a severe tone of voice, grabbing a child, giving a cold look)
(d) Accepts feelings	(e.g., "I can understand why you feel frustrated when you have to clean up and you are still having fun playing.")
(e) Encourages perspective taking	(e.g., "how do you think another child feels when taking you grab something from him/her?")
(f) Encourages independence	(e.g., "If you both want a turn to play with this toy what do you think we should do?")
g.) Addresses personality (May be positive or negative)	(e.g. "You're so lazy, you never help to clean up." "You're so smart.")
h.) Addresses behaviour (May be positive or negative.)	(e.g. "You're doing a great job picking up all the blocks.)

Teacher Practices Observation Scale Coding Sheet

Name of teacher_____ Date_____

Daycare_____ time start_____

time finish_____

	1	2	3	4	5	6	7	8	9	10	11	12
Time-sampled codes												
Contact with children												
small group/one child												
large group												
Without Children												
on-task												
off-task												
Event-Sampled codes												
praise/encouragement												
hostility												
activity participation												
addresses behaviour												

addresses personality												
accepts feelings												
encourages perspective taking												
encourages independence												

Appendix B

<u>Questionnaire</u>

1.) How long have you been working in the Early Childhood Education field?

a.) less than a year   b.) 1-3 years   c.) 4-6 years   d.) 7-10 years   e.) more than ten years

2.) What is your level of education?

    a.) high school leaving certificate
    b.) some CEGEP courses
    c.) completion of D.E.C.
    d.) attestation
    e.) some university courses
    f.) completion of undergraduate program
    g.) graduate program

3.) Why did you choose to work in the field of early childhood education?

4.) How long have you been working at this center?

5.) How many children are in your group?

6.) Does the center have a philosophy? Can you describe it? Do you agree with all
    aspects of the philosophy?

7.) Is there any particular early childhood educational philosophy which you think best
describes your teaching style or beliefs?

8.) How would you describe a typical day in your classroom?

9.) How many free play periods do you have during the day?

    0   1   2   3 or more

10.) How long is the duration of each free play period?

   0-15 min.   16-25 min.   26-45 min.   46-60 min.

11.) Are children allowed to play with any materials they want?   Yes   No

11a.) Why or why not? (please explain)

_____
_____
_____
_____

12a.) Is it alright for children to combine toys/materials (i.e., can children use blocks to build homes for plastic animals?)

                                    Yes   No

12b.) If so, why or why not?

_____
_____
_____

13a.) Are children able to play with the same materials for more than 1 free play period?

   Yes   No

13b.) Why or why not (please explain)

_____
_____
_____

14.) Do you believe that teachers should limit the length of time children can play in one particular area or with certain toys or materials?   Yes   No

Why or why not?

_____
_____
_____

15.) Do you believe that teachers should limit how many children can play in particular corner or participate in an activity?   Yes   No

Why or why not?

_____
_____

16.) Is free play an important part of your program?   Yes   No

Why or why not?

_____

_____

17.) What is your role during free play? What do you do? How do you do it?

_____

_____

Now I am going to read you some statements and I will ask you how much you agree or disagree.

18.) During free play periods it is important for teachers to interact with children

1.) Strongly agree 2.) Agree 3.) Neutral 4.) Disagree 5.) Strongly disagree

Please comment

_____

19.) During free play time it is important for educators to observe children's play from a distance.

1.) Strongly agree 2.) Agree 3.) Neutral 4.) Disagree 5.) Strongly disagree

Please comment

_____

20.) Free play is as important as structured play time.

1.) Strongly agree 2.) Agree 3.) Neutral 4.) Disagree 5.) Strongly disagree

Please comment

_____

21.) How many structured play periods do you have during the average day?

    a.) 0   b.) 1   c.) 2   d.) 3 or more

22.) How much time do you spend in structured activities during the day?

　　　0-15 min.　16-25 min.　　26-45 min.　46 –60 min.　60 min. or more

23.) Describe what you do during a structured activity. What kind of structured activities do you do in your class. Please provide some examples.

_____
_____
_____

24.) Is it important to interact with children during structured play periods? Yes　No

24a.) Why or why not?

_____
_____
_____

25.) Do you preselect materials for children to play with during a structured activity?
　　　Yes　　No

25a.) Why or why not (please explain) if yes, what do you see of the value in this?

_____
_____
_____

26.) Do children need to be told what to do in order to learn?　　Yes　No

Why or why not (please explain)?

_____
_____
_____

27.) When structuring play is it important that all children participate? Yes　No

Why or why not?

_____
_____

27a.) What if they are not interested or don't want to?

_____
_____

Now I am going to read you some statements and I will ask you how much you agree or disagree.

28.) Structuring children's play is the best way to facilitate their learning and prepare them for school.

1.) Strongly agree   2.) Agree   3.) Neutral   4.) Disagree   5.) Strongly Disagree

Please comment

_____
_____
_____

29.) Structuring children's play can limit their creativity and hinder their ability to make choices for themselves.

1.) Strongly agree   2.) Agree   3.) Neutral   4.) Disagree   5.) Strongly Disagree

Please comment

_____
_____
_____

30.) Children need to be given direction. If you allow them to choose what they want to do they will usually play with the same materials repeatedly and this is not good for their development.

1.) Strongly agree   2.) Agree   3.) Neutral   4.) Disagree   5.) Strongly Disagree

Please comment

_____
_____
_____

31.) Should children be left alone to play in they way they choose without adult involvement or should teachers engage themselves in the children's play? Yes   No

Why or why not?

_____
_____
_____

32.) What does it mean to you to guide children's play?

_____
_____
_____

33.) Is it important to guide children's play to help them learn?   Yes   No

Why or why not?

_____
_____

34.) Is there a difference between structuring and guiding children's play? If yes, please explain the difference. Can you give some examples to explain the difference.

_____
_____
_____

35.) What is the best aspect of your program? Examples.

_____
_____
_____
_____

36.) What is the most important part of an early childhood educator's job?

_____
_____
_____
_____

37.) Can you talk about one part of your day that occurred while I was there that was the most meaningful to you?

_____
_____
_____

Thank you for your time